The Strongest Man on Earth

By the Same Author

Novels and Romances

SINISTER STREET
SYLVIA SCARLETT
GUY AND PAULINE
CARNIVAL
FIGURE OF EIGHT
CORAL
THE VANITY GIRL
ROGUES AND VAGABONDS
THE ALTAR STEPS
THE PARSON'S PROGRESS
THE HEAVENLY LADDER
HUNTING THE FAIRIES
WHISKY GALORE
KEEP THE HOME GUARD TURNING
THE MONARCH OF THE GLEN
THE RIVAL MONSTER
THE RED TAPEWORM
ROCKETS GALORE
THE LUNATIC REPUBLIC
POOR RELATIONS
APRIL FOOLS
RICH RELATIVES
BUTTERCUPS AND DAISIES
WATER ON THE BRAIN
VESTAL FIRE
EXTRAORDINARY WOMEN
THIN ICE
EXTREMES MEET
THE THREE COURIERS
OUR STREET
THE DARKENING GREEN
THE PASSIONATE ELOPEMENT
FAIRY GOLD
THE SEVEN AGES OF WOMEN
PARADISE FOR SALE
THE FOUR WINDS OF LOVE:
    THE EAST WIND
    THE SOUTH WIND
    THE WEST WIND
    THE NORTH WIND
MEZZOTINT
THE STOLEN SOPRANO
PAPER LIVES

Play

THE LOST CAUSE

Verse

POEMS 1907
KENSINGTON RHYMES

History and Biography

EASTERN EPIC. VOL. I

ALL OVER THE PLACE
GALLIPOLI MEMORIES
ATHENIAN MEMORIES
GREEK MEMORIES
AEGEAN MEMORIES
WIND OF FREEDOM
MR ROOSEVELT
DR BENES
PRINCE CHARLIE
PRINCE CHARLIE AND HIS LADIES
CATHOLICISM IN SCOTLAND
MARATHON AND SALAMIS
PERICLES
THE WINDSOR TAPESTRY
THE VITAL FLAME
I TOOK A JOURNEY
COALPORT
REALMS OF SILVER
THE QUEEN'S HOUSE
MY RECORD OF MUSIC
SUBLIME TOBACCO
GREECE IN MY LIFE
CATS' COMPANY
CATMINT
LOOK AT CATS

Essays and Criticism

ECHOES
A MUSICAL CHAIR
UNCONSIDERED TRIFLES
REAPED AND BOUND
LITERATURE IN MY TIME
ON MORAL COURAGE

Children's Stories

SANTA CLAUS IN SUMMER
TOLD
MABEL IN QUEER STREET
THE UNPLEASANT VISITORS
THE CONCEITED DOLL
THE ENCHANTED BLANKET
THE DINING-ROOM BATTLE
THE ADVENTURES OF TWO CHAIRS
THE ENCHANTED ISLAND
THE NAUGHTYMOBILE
THE FAIRY IN THE WINDOW BOX
THE STAIRS THAT KEPT ON GOING DOWN

Autobiography

MY LIFE AND TIMES: OCTAVE ONE;
OCTAVE TWO; OCTAVE THREE;
OCTAVE FOUR; OCTAVE FIVE;
OCTAVE SIX

THE STRONGEST MAN ON EARTH

By

Compton Mackenzie

Based on the B.B.C. Television
'Jackanory' programme

Illustrated by T. Ritchie

Chatto and Windus
LONDON

Published by
Chatto & Windus Ltd.
42 William IV Street,
London, W.C.2.

★

Clarke, Irwin & Co., Ltd.,
Toronto

Printed in Great Britain
at the Blackmore Press, Gillingham, Dorset
by T. H. Brickell & Son, Ltd.

TO JOY WHITBY

and all those in that Riverside studio of
the B.B.C. who helped me to tell the story
of Perseus and Theseus in 'Jackanory' and to
the children who wrote me such enchanting
letters after listening to that story.

Contents

CONTENTS

Prologue

IN the month of March 1966 I was one of the people who tell stories to small boys and girls in a B.B.C. series called *Jackanory*. I chose for the stories I would tell the adventures of two heroes of ancient Greece called Perseus and Theseus. I had no idea whether I should be able to make those adventures interesting to the children of to-day, although when I was eight years old I had been fascinated by a book called *The Heroes*, written by Charles Kingsley. To my delight and a good deal to my surprise I had a lot of letters from five-year-olds, six-year-olds, seven-year-olds, eight-year-olds, nine-year-olds, ten-year-olds, and even one or two from twelve-year-olds, asking for more stories about that wonderful land of ancient Greece. So I made up my mind I would try to tell some more stories of that beautiful country, and put them in a book.

I was lucky enough to start learning Greek when I was just nine, but owing to the stupidity of grown-ups hardly anybody to-day starts learning Greek when he or she is nine. I do not have to tell you that grown-ups can be terribly stupid. However, although you may not have been lucky enough to learn Greek, I am going to use the Greek names for the Immortals and mortals in my story, and the story I have chosen is the exciting story of the strongest man on earth, who became an Immortal. His name was Herakles but the Romans called him Hercules. You will have heard people talk of somebody being 'as strong as Hercules' and you will hear sometimes of a 'Herculean effort' applied to a task of tremendous difficulty.

Before I begin I think it would help you to follow his adventures if I tried to give you some idea of the world as it was when Herakles came into it. Compared with the world in which you and I live to-day it was a very small world. When, three thousand years hence, writers tell children about our world to-day it will seem much smaller to them than their own vast world of the future. People flying about among the planets and stars will smile to read what an adventure it once seemed to fly even as far as the moon.

To the Hellenes, as the people who had conquered ancient Greece were called, and are still called by the people of modern Greece, Hellas was the centre of that small world. They thought of it as flat, and surrounded by Ocean, which flowed round it like a mighty and mysterious river. On a map of to-day it would include the Mediterranean sea, the easterly coast of Spain, the southerly coast of France, Italy, Egypt, Morocco, Asia Minor, the Black Sea, Palestine and western Arabia.

Hellas itself was divided up into small city-states, each of which was ruled by a king, and in all these city-states the people worshipped the Twelve Gods and Goddesses whose abode was Mount Olympus toward the north of Hellas. The supreme god was Zeus, the father of gods and men. When he and his two brothers Poseidon and Pluto drove out their father Kronos, whose other name was Saturn, they drew lots for which part of the world each should rule. The sky came to Zeus, the sea to Poseidon, and the world under the earth to Pluto. The earth itself was shared by them. The Romans called Zeus 'Jupiter' or 'Jove'. After all these years we still say 'By Jove!' The Romans called Poseidon 'Neptune'. Pluto did not feast on Olympus with the Twelve; he remained always in that dark underworld called Hades.

Zeus was armed with thunderbolts and when the lightning flashed and the thunder roared the Hellenes believed that it was the voice of Zeus in anger. The wife of Zeus was Hera ('Juno' to the Romans), who was powerful and kind to the heroes she cared for but terribly unkind to other heroes, as you will hear in the tale of Herakles. Hera was the mother of Ares and Hephaistos. Ares, whom the Romans called 'Mars', was the god of war; Hephaistos, whom the Romans called 'Vulcan', was the god of the smithy. He could make anything in his smithy. He once made some golden mechanical men to help him at his work, and a set of three-legged tables that used to run errands for him. It is a good thing that Hephaistos is no longer on Mount Olympus. Otherwise he would probably be making computers that walked about all over the place. The other child of Zeus and Hera was Hebe, who used to carry round the cups of nectar; all we know is that honey was part of it. Honey was also used in the ambrosia that they ate.

Aphrodite, the goddess of love, whom the Romans called

'Venus', was born from the foam of the sea and came ashore at Paphos in the island of Cyprus. Zeus gave her to Hephaistos as his wife. He was ugly and lame and disagreeable; it was not a happy marriage.

Now we come to Apollo, and Artemis whom the Romans called 'Diana'. Zeus was their father; Leto was their mother. They were born on the little island of Delos, in the middle of those islands in the Aegean Sea called the Cyclades. Apollo was the god of archery, of music and of medicine, and the statues of him that remain always show him as a handsome young man. His sister Artemis, the Virgin Huntress, was the goddess of all wild life.

Pallas Athene sprang from the head of Zeus armed with helmet, sword and shield. The Romans called her 'Minerva'. Neither she nor Artemis ever married. Athene helped many of the heroes, and luckily for Herakles she was able to help him as you will hear. Grey-eyed Athene was the patron deity of Athens. That glorious temple on the Acropolis called the Parthenon (Virgin) was sacred to her.

The last of the five goddesses on Olympus was Demeter, the corn goddess, whom the Romans called 'Ceres'. She was the mother of Persephone, whom Pluto stole from her to become his queen of the Underworld. The Romans called her 'Proserpine'.

There are two gods still to mention. Hermes, called 'Mercury' by the Romans, was the son of Zeus and Maia. Maia was a daughter of the Titan Atlas. The Titans were a race of gods older than the Olympian gods, by whom they were overthrown.

Prologue

Hermes was the messenger of Zeus. He had winged sandals which could carry him anywhere, and an adamantine sword which could cut through anything. He was the patron of commerce and any business connected with money, and therefore also the patron of thieves. Finally there was Dionysos or Bacchus, the god of wine, who was the son of Zeus and Semele, a mortal maid. When Dionysos was deified by his father Zeus, Hestia or 'Vesta' as the Romans called her, the goddess of the hearth and home, withdrew from Olympus.

These old Olympian gods may seem very far away from us today, but we still use their names. We still talk of a 'jovial' person, just as we say somebody is 'mercurial'. I am writing these lines on a Saturday and Saturday is Saturn's day, the father of Zeus. We should not have Olympic games if the gods had not once dwelt upon Olympus. Poseidon who ruled the sea had a palace under the water in the stables of which he kept white horses with golden manes to drive his chariot, and to-day we still call breaking waves 'white horses'.

The twelve gods and goddesses on Olympus were the supreme Immortals, but there were many other immortal beings in Hellas once upon a time. There were the nine Muses, who first inspired men to write poetry and music and history, tragic plays and comic plays. Their father was Zeus and their mother was Mnemosyne or Memory. There were beautiful nymphs, for ever young, who were the spirits of nature and were often the mothers of heroes. Those who roamed the mountains, always singing or dancing, were called Oreads, and those in the rivers and streams were Naiads. The trees were haunted by Dryads, many of whom faded away when their trees died. In the sea were the Nereids whom we can think of as like our mermaids, although they did not have fishes' tails.

I could go on telling you story after story from Greek mythology but it is time to begin the tale of the strongest man on earth. Yet there is one god I must mention, because those of you who love pop songs and the dancing that goes with them have to thank the god Pan for it.

Pan's chief haunt was Arcadia, which was the country in the heart of the southern half of Hellas and became the name for any perfect countryside. Nowadays, as the years go by, Arcadia is becoming more and more difficult to find. Perhaps when you are my age it will not exist anywhere, and in our island of Britain there will be scarcely any birds left except pigeons, sparrows and starlings, no moths except clothes-moths, and butterflies will seem as rare as fairies.

Pan was only half human in appearance; the lower part of him was like a goat. He used to enjoy frightening people suddenly, and to-day we still talk about getting into a panic about something. I think he probably enjoyed suddenly frightening people when they were wandering around because he felt that they were be-having like the people to-day who leave paper and bottles about when they picnic in the country. If Pan were still to be seen on earth I should blame him for the stupid way motorists behave and

6

the equally stupid way pedestrians behave and think their stupidity was due to panic. Pan would have hated to hear motor-horns drowning his pipes.

It was Pan who invented the pipe, and this is how it happened. He fell in love with a beautiful dryad called Syrinx, but she thought he was so ugly that she ran away from him and jumped into a river where the naiads turned her into a bed of reeds. Pan realised that she had escaped him but he wanted to keep fresh the memory of beautiful Syrinx. So he cut seven of those reeds and made of them the Pan-pipe, on which he used to play tunes for the Arcadian shepherds and shepherdesses to dance to. Pan once fell in love with another nymph called Echo and the mention of Echo's name reminds me that it is time to begin the tale of Herakles. You will know why presently.

The Birth of Herakles

A MPHITRYON was king of Tiryns, one of the smaller city-states in the Peloponnese, which is the southern half of Hellas almost separated from the northern half by the Gulf of Corinth. The chief city-state of Argolis, in part of the Peloponnese, was Mycenae. Elektryon was king of Mycenae and Amphitryon was married to his lovely daughter Alkmene. When Elektryon had to go to war he left his son-in-law as regent of Mycenae. In that war all the eight sons of Elektryon were killed. On his return he considered making Amphitryon his heir, and then a most unfortunate thing happened. Amphitryon and his father-in-law were walking up and down in a field, talking about local affairs. A cow which had strayed from the herd kept mooing loudly and by her mooing made it impossible for them to hear one another clearly. Amphitryon in a fit of irritation threw a club at the cow to drive her away. He must have thrown it very hard indeed because it hit one of the cow's long horns and rebounding from it caught Elektryon on the side of his head and killed him.

Elektryon had a brother called Sthenelos who seized the opportunity to proclaim himself King of Mycenae and banished Amphitryon from Argolis to Thebes in northern Hellas.

There King Kreon received him kindly and he was purified of

the fatal accident to Elektryon. Whenever a Hellene killed somebody, even accidentally, it was necessary for him to go through a solemn purification. In return Amphitryon helped Kreon to defeat his enemies and we can be glad to know that Alkmene quite understood that her father's death had been an accident.

While Amphitryon was away fighting, Zeus, the father of gods and men, fell in love with the beautiful Alkmene and decided to give her a son who should grow up to be the greatest hero of all the Hellenes.

Hera, the Queen of the Sky, used to get angry and jealous when Zeus fell in love with mortal women. She used to be called ox-eyed Hera by those who worshipped her, and those great eyes of hers were always on the look out when Zeus left Olympus to wander about on the earth below. So Zeus ordered the nymph Echo, who was a wonderful story-teller, to keep Hera occupied listening to her tales while he was away. Pan was very much in love with Echo, but Echo herself would have nothing to do with him because she was in love with a beautiful youth called Narcissus.

When Hera discovered that Echo had been used by Zeus to keep her occupied listening to her stories she was furious with the nymph and deprived her of being able to say anything except the last word or two of what was spoken to her by somebody else. Poor Echo! The next time she saw Narcissus she went to greet him but she could not tell him how much she loved him and Narcissus pushed her away.

9

B

"You annoy me," he said.

"You annoy me," Echo replied.

This upset Narcissus who was very vain.

"Get out of my sight," he shouted.

"Out of my sight," Echo answered back.

Narcissus took her at her word and went off. She pined away for love of him and at last all that was left of her was her voice echoing.

As for Narcissus he wandered about in the woods until he came to a small lake. Kneeling down beside it to drink he saw his own reflection and thought he was so beautiful that he fell in love with himself, so much in love that he could not tear himself away from admiring himself. He remained gazing down into the water day after day until at last he died of exhaustion and self-pity, when he was turned into the flower we call narcissus. Lots of people in the world to-day still fall in love with themselves, and the world would be a sweeter place if such people could all be turned into flowers.

On the day that his son was to be born Zeus did a very stupid thing. He went about Olympus boasting that a child would be born of the blood of Zeus who should be High King of Mycenae and lord over all in Argolis.

Hera was indignant enough at hearing that, but when Zeus told her that he intended to call this child Herakles she was so furiously angry that she made up her mind to spoil her husband's plan. It happened that a child was to be born on the same day to

Menippe, the wife of Sthenelos, who was also of the blood of Zeus.

Hera asked Zeus if he would swear by Styx that the child with his blood first to be born that day would be High King of Mycenae and lord of all those in Argolis around him. Zeus agreed and took the oath. Now, if a god swore an oath by Styx, which is one of the five rivers of Hades, the underworld, he could never break that oath. Then Hera managed to get Menippe's child born an hour before Herakles arrived with his twin brother, Iphikles, the son of Amphitryon. Zeus could not go back on his oath and so Eurystheus, as the son of Menippe was to be called, would have to become High King of Mycenae one day and lord of all those in Argolis around him. You will hear what that was going to cost Herakles when he grew up. He was to find out in a strange way. Moreover, throughout his life on earth he was to suffer from Hera's enmity.

Zeus was naturally angry when he found out how Hera had tricked him into taking that oath and thereby robbed his infant son of his inheritance. He was still determined that Herakles should be the greatest hero of them all, and he never stopped boasting of his great future. So when Herakles was about a year old Hera decided to destroy him.

One night Alkmene put Herakles and his twin brother Iphikles in their cradle under a lamb's-wool blanket and left them asleep in the nursery. Hera sent two large serpents covered with blue scales to coil themselves round the twins and choke the life

out of them. It was midnight when the serpents reached Amphitryon's house in Thebes. The gates opened for them silently and the serpents went gliding into the courtyard and through the door of the house, which opened silently for them to glide on across the marble floors of room after room, until finally they glided into the nursery.

Zeus by now knew what was happening and magically lit up the room, so that the twins awoke to see the blue serpents above their cradle with flames shooting from their eyes, their forked tongues darting in and out as they prepared to curl themselves round the two babies and choke them to death. Iphikles gave a shrill scream and rolled out of the cradle on to the floor in terror; there he lay, screaming and screaming. The noise woke up his mother and when she saw the light shining under the door of the nursery she woke up Amphitryon, who leapt out of bed and seized his sword, which was hanging beside it. The light in the nursery went out at that moment and he shouted for slaves to bring lamps. When he entered the nursery he saw Herakles sitting up in the cradle chortling away with a broad smile on his chubby face. He had a serpent in each hand and was squeezing the life out of it. As Amphitryon ran along to help, Herakles flung the dead serpents at his feet. Then jumping up and down in his cradle he laughed with glee while Alkmene was trying to comfort Iphikles, who was still sobbing with fright. Amphitryon put back the lamb's-wool blanket over Herakles, who at once went quietly to sleep.

Zeus was naturally very angry with Hera for trying to kill Herakles with those blue serpents; so angry indeed that he threatened to hang her up by the arms with a heavy weight attached to her feet, a punishment that was sometimes given to slaves who misbehaved themselves. Hera did not try to injure Herakles again for a long time, but she still hated him and one day she would do a most terrible thing to him, as you will hear.

The Growing Up of Herakles

As soon as Herakles was old enough his education began. He was given the best teachers for astronomy and philosophy, and we hear that he worked hard at his lessons; but the ancient Greeks thought that any young hero should pay as much attention to his body as to his mind. Amphitryon was a good chariot-driver, and he took a great deal of trouble teaching Herakles to drive a chariot as well as himself; it gave him much pleasure to see the way his pupil took his two horses round the racecourse without ever losing his balance. He was taught wrestling and boxing and fencing and excelled at them all, but what he enjoyed most was the lessons he received in archery from one of Amphitryon's herdsmen, who was a Scythian.

The Scythians, who came from beyond the Black Sea, were the best archers in the world. They drew the arrow in the bow back to their ears, whereas other archers drew it only as far as their chests. It was not until the time of the famous long-bowmen of England that the equals of Scythian archers were found. In Hellas long ago Herakles became the most famous archer in the world, and he could fling the javelin harder and with better aim than any other hero.

Herakles was taught music by Eumolpos, who was a grandson

of Apollo himself. Music included playing the lyre and the flute and also singing. It was over a music lesson that Herakles got into serious trouble. One day Eumolpos was unable to give him his lesson and Linos, under whom he was studying literature, took the place of Eumolpos. Linos did not know nearly as much about music but he was conceited and began to contradict what Eumolpos had been teaching his young pupil. Herakles argued the point; Linos lost his temper and started to give Herakles a beating, whereupon Herakles hit Linos on the head with his lyre and killed him. He had not meant to kill him but he really did not know his own strength.

Well, of course, Herakles was in heavy trouble. In fact he was tried for murder, although at this date he could not have been much more than fifteen years old. Yet he pleaded his own case and quoted a law which said that murder was not murder if committed in self-defence.

However, Amphitryon thought it would be wise to keep him out of further mischief for a while and sent him away to pasture his cattle in the upland valleys. By the time he reached eighteen Herakles was six feet tall. This does not sound so very tall to us, but you must remember that the Hellenic heroes were usually much shorter than that.

While Herakles was pasturing the flocks and herds of Amphitryon, a lion was doing a good deal of damage. Herakles set out to track it down, and at last he killed it with a club which he cut from a wild-olive tree on Mount Helikon. Soon after this, King

Kreon of Thebes was at war and in battle after battle Herakles was conspicuous for his valour and skill. In one fight Amphitryon his foster-father was killed, which was a great grief to Herakles.

King Kreon had been so much impressed by the young hero's conduct as a warrior that he rewarded him by giving him his daughter Megara in marriage, and by her Herakles had two children. He was living happily with her, held in high esteem by everybody, when an appalling calamity befell him.

The Madness of Herakles

WHAT it was that rekindled Hera's hatred of Herakles we do not know. Perhaps Zeus boasted about his heroic son and talked of the future immortality he had in mind for him. Anyway, Hera's hatred of Herakles *was* rekindled and she determined to drive him mad.

One day the small sons of Herakles were playing at soldiers, and Hera made their father, who was coming back from some war, imagine that they were the enemy he had just been fighting. He shot one of them with an arrow from his bow, and was aiming an arrow at the other when Megara, rushing out to protect her other little son, received the arrow in her heart. Yet the madness still raged and Herakles shot his second son.

Then the madness with which Hera had set his brain on fire was quenched and you can imagine what Herakles felt when he looked down at the bodies of his wife and young sons and realised what he had done in the belief that he was being attacked by armed enemies. Overcome by grief, he shut himself in a pitch-dark cellar underground. While he was suffering the pangs of remorse his father Zeus put into his head the idea that, after he had been purified of his terrible deed, he should ask the Oracle at Delphi what he must do to atone for what he had done in his madness.

The Madness of Herakles

The story went that once upon a time Zeus, being anxious to know exactly where the centre of the earth was, sent two eagles to fly from either end of it. They met above Delphi and the stone on which they alighted was accepted as the centre of the earth. This stone was called the Omphalos, which is the Greek word for 'navel'. It was guarded by a dragon called Python; before the birth of Zeus's children Apollo and Artemis, Hera, who was jealous of their mother Leto, sent the Python to frighten her into taking refuge on the floating isle of Delos. Hera was hoping that this island would float away with Leto and be lost in the great stream Okeanos that flowed around the world. However, Zeus asked his brother Poseidon, god of the sea, to anchor it; so Delos became like other islands and never floated about any more.

Soon after Apollo was born he set out to kill the Python, which he did. Then he learned prophecy from the god Pan and inspired a priestess called the Pythoness or Pythia to utter his prophetic advice to those who came to consult the Delphic Oracle. The Pythoness herself had to be an old maid of over fifty. She sat on a tripod and went into a kind of trance when she was receiving inspiration from Apollo. Her oracular utterances were usually interpretations, and if the consultant made a mistake he was blamed for misunderstanding what the Oracle had said to him.

To-day the site of the Oracle Delphi is covered with fascinating ruins and half-ruins that have survived from the days of its influence on human affairs. The view from them is the most beautiful view I have ever seen, and I hope that many of you will see Delphi for yourselves one day, mountains and valleys and streams all around, haunted once upon a time by gods and nymphs and heroes, and haunted to-day by history.

The motto Apollo gave to his sacred fane was 'Know Thyself', and if only the men and women of to-day could follow that divine command a little more successfully than the men and women of the past, our world would not be in the muddle it is in.

You will remember that Tiryns was the original kingdom of Amphitryon; Herakles after his madness in Thebes wanted to return there. Therefore when the Pythia told him to go to Tiryns he was glad at first, but he was not so glad when she told him he must serve Eurystheus for twelve years, and that no matter what tasks Eurystheus set him he must perform those tasks if he hoped to achieve the immortality that his father Zeus had planned for him.

Herakles went away much depressed by the Oracle's advice. There was Eurystheus enjoying the inheritance Herakles was to have had, because Hera had tricked Zeus into taking that rash oath and then managed to ensure that Eurystheus should be born an hour before him. For a while Herakles could not bring himself to put himself under the commands of a man so much inferior to himself in every way, but knowing as he did that the Pythia at Delphi was telling him what Zeus wished him to do, he at last brought himself to go to Tiryns, and from there to Mycenae, where Eurystheus was High King in the palace that he felt ought to have been his own. You can imagine how pleased Eurystheus was when Herakles arrived and put himself at his service and began what were called the Twelve Labours of Herakles.

Eurystheus was really a most unpleasant man. One might think that he would have had a little sympathy with Herakles, but apparently he had none. He delighted in rubbing in the fact that Herakles was his servant. He had not even the decency to tell Herakles personally what his next Labour was to be. He used to send a herald to tell him. Moreover, originally there were to have been Ten Labours; but Eurystheus refused to accept two of them as having been performed and so there were Twelve Labours.

It is pleasant to be able to say that, whatever meanness and malice Eurystheus showed to Herakles, some of the gods on Olympus wished him well in his hope of achieving the divine immortality his father Zeus desired for him. Hermes gave him a sword and Apollo gave him one of his own bows, with arrows feathered with eagle's feathers. Hephaistos gave him bronze greaves and an adamantine helmet hammered in his own smithy on Olympus. Athene gave him a golden breastplate, which she probably persuaded Hephaistos to make for Herakles by reminding him that Ares, the god of war, was inclined to be jealous of the prowess of Herakles in war. Hephaistos was always glad to annoy Ares, because his wife Aphrodite was too fond of him for his liking. Athene herself was always quite pleased to annoy Hera. Finally Poseidon gave Herakles a team of his famous white horses from his stables under the sea.

Iolaos, the son of Herakles' twin brother Iphikles, volunteered to accompany Herakles as his chariot-driver and squire.

The first Labour that Eurystheus imposed on Herakles was to slay and flay the Nemean lion. We call them the 'Labours' of Herakles because the Romans translated the Greek word wrongly. The Greek word for them was 'athloi' from which we get our words 'athletic' and 'athlete'. The Labours of Herakles are really athletic achievements of the strongest and most agile man on earth.

The Nemean Lion

HERAKLES did not take Iolaos with him but set out confidently alone in search of the Nemean lion, which had its headquarters in a cave with two entrances on Mount Tretos, near the city of Nemea in the northern Peloponnese. Herakles had successfully tracked and killed a lion on Mount Helikon when he was only eighteen. He had killed that lion with a club cut from a wild-olive tree. Now he was armed with weapons given to him by some of the Olympian gods. He was inclined at first to disbelieve people when they told him that this lion was an enormous beast with a skin that could not be penetrated by arrow, spear or sword, and that it had already carried off many shepherds in the countryside round its cave to eat them inside.

On his way to Nemea Herakles came to the house of a shepherd called Molorchos, outside the little city of Kleonai between Corinth and Argos. Molorchos told him that the lion had just killed his son and that he was preparing to sacrifice a ram to propitiate Queen Hera.

"To propitiate Hera!" Herakles exclaimed. "What has Hera got to do with this lion?"

"All say that it was Queen Hera who brought him here. It's a monster, not an ordinary lion."

When he heard this Herakles knew Hera was hoping that his first Labour would be his last, and that he would be deprived of the divine immortality promised him by his father Zeus.

"Don't sacrifice a ram to Hera," he told Molorchos. "Wait for me to return in thirty days and we will both sacrifice to Zeus the Saviour."

"But if you do not return in thirty days?" Molorchos asked.

"If I do not return, then sacrifice to me as a hero," Herakles told him proudly.

It was about noon of the next day when Herakles reached Nemea and looked about for somebody to tell him the best way to find the lion's cave. He could not see anybody and supposed that the heat of the midday sun had driven them all indoors; but when he knocked at various doors there was no answer. At last a door was opened by an old woman, who told him the lion had killed and eaten so many of the people of Nemea that the city had been abandoned for the time being.

Herakles had reached the last but one of those thirty days, wandering all over the mountains in search of the lion's lair. At last, when he was beginning to give up hope of finding his quarry, he saw the huge beast come back to its cave, its fur stained here and there with blood from the day's slaughter. Herakles took an arrow from the quiver given to him by Apollo and pulling the string back to his ear let fly. The arrow just rebounded from the lion's skin, and so did half a dozen more which Herakles shot at the monster. The lion simply stretched itself and yawned.

c

Herakles now drew the sword given to him by Hermes and with a fierce sweep slashed at the lion's neck, but the sword bent back without making the slightest impression. Luckily for Herakles he had cut himself another club out of a wild-olive tree on his way up Mount Tretos. He raised it above his head and brought it down with such a tremendous thump on the lion's nose that his club was broken. Instead of springing at its assailant the lion retreated into its cave, shaking its head. Herakles was glad to have given the lion so much pain; in fact he had not hurt the lion at all; he had merely deafened him with the blow.

Herakles did not worry about his broken club; he realised that the monster was proof against any weapons. He decided that the only way he could overcome his adversary was by wrestling with it. So into the cave he went and a terrific wrestle began, in the course of which the lion bit off one of Herakles's fingers. At last Herakles got the lion's head under his arm and squeezed and squeezed its neck so hard that he squeezed the life out of the monster.

When Herakles, carrying the carcass of the Nemean lion, arrived back at Kleonai it was almost the end of the thirtieth day, and he found Molorchos preparing to sacrifice to him as a hero.

"No, no, my friend," he said. "You and I must now sacrifice to Zeus the Saviour."

You can imagine how gratified Zeus was by the triumph of Herakles over the Nemean lion.

The hero picked up the carcass and when he arrived with it in

Mycenae the cowardly King Eurystheus was so frightened by it that he hid himself.

The next problem for Herakles was how to flay the lion, because the task set by Eurystheus for his First Labour was to slay *and* flay the Nemean lion. He tried every kind of instrument but that invulnerable skin blunted them all. Meanwhile the wretched Eurystheus had ordered his smiths to make him a large bronze urn, which was buried in the earth and into which Eurystheus planned to retire whenever Herakles's arrival in Mycenae was announced.

Herakles prayed to the gods to tell him how to flay the carcass of the Nemean lion, and it may have been Athene who put it into his head to skin the carcass with its own claws. It was a most successful operation. Herakles made of the skin the equivalent of a suit of armour no mortal weapon could pierce, and for an equally impenetrable helmet he wore the lion's head upon his own. No doubt it was Herakles's appearance in the lion's skin that made Eurystheus scuttle away and hide himself in his urn. From there he sent his herald to order Herakles to undertake, as his Second Labour, the destruction of the Lernaean Hydra.

The Lernaean Hydra

THE great swamp of Lerna began some five miles north of Argos and was close to the sea. Above it was Mount Pontinos, on which was a grove of sacred plane-trees which went on down beside the swamp to the sea. Where a river rose under the roots of a plane-tree at the edge of the swamp was the lair of the hydra, which was an enormous creature with a body shaped like that of a dog and about ten heads at the end of necks as long as snakes. One of these heads was immortal.

The swamp was unfathomable and it was believed that the hydra devoured unfortunate travellers who sank into it. I think it is reasonable to suppose that once upon a time lakes and swamps really were the haunt of prehistoric monsters. How otherwise are we to explain the tales we are told of such monsters in Irish, Welsh and Scottish mythology? In the Highlands of Scotland they were called kelpies or water-horses. The word 'hydra' means a watery animal. Many people to-day are convinced that there is an enormous prehistoric monster in Loch Ness. Some of the descriptions I have heard from people who claim to have seen it sound not unlike the hydra.

The goddess Athene had a shrine not far from the Lernaean swamp and was anxious to help Herakles when he drove there in the chariot with his nephew Iolaos. Armoured by the skin and head of the Nemean lion, Herakles felt confident of eluding the hydra's fangs; but Athene warned him that the very breath of the hydra was fatally poisonous and that when he came to grips with the monster he must hold his own breath.

The next problem was to make the hydra come out of its lair and Athene prompted Herakles to pelt it with burning arrows. Then when it came right out she advised Herakles to seize it with his strong arms, and to be sure to hold his breath while he battered the life out of one head after another with his club. This may have been good advice but as soon as Herakles approached the hydra it coiled its heads round his feet and nearly tripped him up. Moreover, as fast as he battered the life out of one head two more appeared in its place. Then Hera, who had been angry with Athene for trying to help Herakles, sent an enormous crab out of the swamp to help the hydra. It caught one of Herakles' feet in its huge claws, but with the other foot he stamped so hard upon the crab that he crushed its shell and its claws could no longer hold his foot.

Herakles now shouted to Iolaos to set fire to a corner of the sacred grove and, in order to stop the hydra from growing new heads, to burn their roots with blazing bunches and so prevent the blood from flowing. Herakles then took his sword and cut off the hydra's immortal head. It was still hissing at him when he buried it beneath a heavy rock beside the road. Then Herakles dipped his arrows in the monster's blood, which would make any

wound from them fatal. These poisoned arrows he put in his quiver for use in emergency.

Eurystheus argued that Herakles could not count the killing of the Lernaean hydra as a properly performed Labour because Iolaos had helped him. However, he lost no time in getting Herakles away from Mycenae by sending him to capture or kill the Keryneian hind.

The Keryneian Hind

WHEN the goddess Artemis was a child she saw five hinds grazing beside the banks of a river in Thessaly. They had golden antlers like a stag's and bronze hooves and were much bigger than any hinds Artemis had seen. She was captivated by their grace and beauty and made up her mind to harness them to her chariot. When they saw Artemis running after them the hinds ran too but they were not fast enough to escape the Virgin Huntress. One after another she caught four of them and harnessed them to her chariot, but the fifth hind escaped and took refuge in the Keryneian hills in Arcadia. Artemis ruled that this hind should be held sacred to her and no hunter ventured to attack it.

When Hera put it into the head of Eurystheus to set for the Third Labour of Herakles the task of bringing the Keryneian hind dead or alive to Mycenae she no doubt hoped to involve Herakles with Artemis. However, the hero was too wise to anger the goddess by killing or wounding her sacred hind, and he set his heart on capturing the animal alive.

For a whole year he hunted her all over the known world, even as far northward as the land of the Hyperboreans. Some have suggested that the Keryneian hind was in fact a reindeer. Cer-

tainly only the hinds of reindeer have antlers and only reindeer can be harnessed.

At long last, when the hind had been pursued by Herakles back to Arcadia, she took refuge at the foot of Mount Artemision from which she came to fall asleep under an apple-tree beside a river, utterly exhausted. Herakles crept up as quietly as he could, put a net over the hind and after tying her legs placed her over his shoulders and set off to Mycenae as fast as possible.

On the way he was met by Artemis, who demanded sternly why he had been hunting her sacred hind.

Herakles was not at all anxious to make an enemy of Artemis.

"I knew well that this hind was sacred to you, goddess. But when Queen Hera put it into the head of Eurystheus to demand the Keryneian hind, dead or alive, as my Third Labour I had to obey. The Oracle of your brother Apollo at Delphi commanded me to expiate the crimes I committed in the madness Queen Hera cast upon me, by obeying the orders of Eurystheus for twelve years to come. I have done my utmost not to hurt your sacred hind, goddess, and I vow that as soon as I have shown her to Eurystheus I will set her free to roam wherever you bid her roam."

The Virgin Huntress was mollified by Herakles's explanation.

"Carry my sacred hind to Mycenae and when you have shown her to Eurystheus set her free."

Herakles bent his knees in grateful worship of the goddess and went on his way.

As soon as he had shown Eurystheus that his Third Labour had been accomplished he released the sacred hind and was set for his fourth task, the capture alive of the Erymanthian boar.

The Erymanthian Boar

THIS huge beast had become a threat to the country of Arcadia. It fed in the thickets of Mount Lampeia and among the holm-oaks and pines of Mount Erymanthos, but it used often to come rooting about along the banks of the river Erymanthos and whenever it met any of the country folk it used to attack them and gash them fatally with its large, savage tusks.

Herakles in the impenetrable skin of the Nemean lion was not in the least afraid of the boar's tusks, and the boar itself seemed to know this, because it hid itself high up on Mount Erymanthos. Herakles shouted and shouted, and so loud was his voice that the boar came out of a thicket and went galloping up the mountain until it galloped into a deep snow drift where Herakles overtook it and jumped on its back. Then he bound the boar with chains and set out to carry it on his shoulders all the way to Mycenae. On the road there he heard news of the gathering of the Argonauts, and when he reached Mycenae he flung the chained boar down at the entrance to the market place and without waiting for Eurystheus to tell him what his next Labour was he set out for Pagasae, where the great ship *Argo* had been built and the heroes were all gathering for the famous voyage to Colchis in search of the Golden Fleece. Herakles took with him as his squire to carry his bow and arrows a handsome youth called Hylas.

The Argonauts

No wonder Herakles was not going to let his bondage to
Eurystheus prevent his being one of those fifty heroes who
answered Jason's call to join the crew of the first voyage of a
longship from Hellas. And this is how that voyage came about.

When Kretheus, the King of Iolkos in Thessaly, died he left a
son called Aeson and a stepson, whose father was Poseidon, called
Pelias. Pelias usurped the throne and said he would act as
guardian of his nephew Jason; he had no heir himself. Jason's
mother, Philyra, did not trust Pelias and she smuggled her son
away and put him in charge of the centaur Cheiron who lived in a
cave at the head of a glen on the great mountain Pelion. Unlike
most centaurs Cheiron was wise and kind; he was also skilled in
music and in medicine. He was the tutor of many princely heroes
who were sent from all over Hellas to be educated by him. When
Jason grew up he set out to find what was happening in Iolkos. On
his way from Cheiron's cave he saw beside a swollen stream an
old woman who evidently wanted to cross to the other side but
was afraid. Jason lifted her up and carried her across, but it had
been quite a job to struggle over against the torrent and in the
course of that struggle he lost one of his sandals in the mud.

When Jason put the old woman gently down on the opposite

bank he found himself in front of a beautiful and majestic woman who was gazing at him with her great eyes. She thanked Jason for his help and told him that henceforth she would always befriend him.

Jason bowed his knees in worship, for this was none other than Queen Hera herself. It is rather a relief to find that Hera, who had been such a bitter enemy of Herakles, was going to be the friend of another hero.

Jason went on his way to Iolkos and Pelias was not at all pleased to see his nephew, because an oracle had warned him against a man with one sandal who would also be a kinsman. So Pelias decided that for his own safety Jason was better away from Iolkos. If you look in a map of modern Greece you can see a place called Volo, and if you ever go to Greece you will be able to visit what was once Iolkos and what is still Mount Pelion.

Pelias told Jason that every night the ghost of Phrixos was appearing to him and asking for the Golden Fleece to be brought back to Thessaly. He had sacrificed the ram to Zeus and hung up the fleece itself in a dragon-guarded grove by Colchis on the Black Sea.

It is a little difficult to understand why Jason should have paid so much attention to the ghost of Phrixos. Probably the explanation is that Jason welcomed the adventure and thought many other heroes would welcome it equally. The ship was called the *Argo* because it was designed by a hero called Argos. Not only did Hera help with her advice but also Athene. The latter goddess even brought a piece of oaken wood from the Oracle of Zeus at Dodona to fix in the bows, and this piece of wood had the power of speech and prophecy. Dodona was the oldest oracle of all in Hellas in its remote and mysterious grove of holm-oaks. At last the *Argo*, built with twenty-five benches for a pair of oars on each, was ready to sail.

Herakles arrived just before the *Argo* was launched at Pagasae, the harbour of Iolkos, and went up to visit his old tutor Cheiron, who had the body of a tawny horse and the arms and chest of a man, and whose head was as noble a head as could be seen anywhere. Herakles walked on through the thick oak wood, above which were pine woods, until he reached the centaur's cave. Cheiron came out of it to greet his visitor, and riding on his back was the boy Achilles, who was playing to himself on a lyre. His father Peleus was one of the Argonauts.

Cheiron looked at the club and lion's skin of Herakles.

"Man worthy of such arms and arms worthy of such a man," he observed.

The young Achilles could not resist prodding the bristles of the lion's skin, and while he was doing this Cheiron was looking at Herakles's quiver.

And then a sad thing happened; one of the arrows fell out and stuck in Cheiron's leg just above his hoof. The poison from the blood of the Lernaean hydra began its deadly work at once. Cheiron groaned as he drew the arrow out; Herakles and young Achilles groaned too. Cheiron, who was a master of herbal

39

remedies, tried to assuage the wound with poultices. It was no use; the poison defied every remedy. The noble centaur was obviously in agony and as he lay upon the ground outside his cave the boy Achilles fondled his hands that were growing ever feebler, and wept.

"Do not leave me, dear father," he begged, but as Achilles bent over to kiss him the noble centaur died and Zeus set him among the stars.

The mother of Achilles was the sea-queen Thetis. While he was an infant his mother dipped him in the Styx to make him invulnerable. She held him by the heel which was therefore the only part of him that remained vulnerable. One day Achilles would be killed by an arrow in his heel.

The renown of Herakles was already great when he joined the Argonauts, and at the banquet to celebrate the launching of the *Argo* he was unanimously acclaimed leader of the expedition.

But Herakles said: "I do not wish such an honour. I will not command this ship. Let the hero who brought us together from all over Hellas command us."

This generous recognition of Jason's achievement was echoed by the other heroes, and after that nobody questioned Jason's leadership. Lots were drawn to decide which two oarsmen should occupy each bench. Herakles and Ankaios, the two strongest of the heroes, sat together on the middle bench, and in the first grey of dawn the *Argo* sailed from Pagasae, her course set for the island of Lemnos, the first port of call. The wind, which had been

41

favourable so far, died down as the ship drew near to Lemnos and the Argonauts had to take to their oars.

When the ship drew nearer to Lemnos the Argonauts were amazed to see a number of women in armour lined up along the shore to resist their landing. A year or two before this, the women of Lemnos had neglected to pay proper reverence to the goddess Aphrodite. Her husband Hephaistos had one of his smithies in an extinct volcano on Lemnos, and naturally Aphrodite expected to be treated with proper respect by the Lemnian women. So to give them a lesson Aphrodite made them all smell so unpleasantly that their husbands could not bear their company and used to go over to Thrace and spend their time with the Thracian young women. The women of Lemnos plotted together and one dreadful night they murdered every male on the island.

When they sighted the *Argo* the Lemnian women had supposed it was a ship from Thrace carrying men to avenge the massacre. Jason sent a herald to explain that he and his fellow heroes had come as friends not as enemies. The women by now were quite glad to see some men about again, and the Queen Hypsipyle invited them to come ashore. They were so well entertained that the Argonauts might never have continued their quest of the Golden Fleece but for Herakles. He had stayed on board the *Argo*, being looked after by his squire Hylas. At last he grew tired of waiting about for the rest of the Argonauts and went ashore to ask them if they had forgotten they had set out in quest of the Golden Fleece. Were they going to waste any more time amusing themselves in Lemnos? Herakles's rebuke had its effect. In spite of the entreaties of the Lemnian women to stay longer the Argonauts set sail.

After visiting the island of Samothrace it was necessary for the *Argo* to pass through the Hellespont, or as we call it to-day the Dardanelles. Tiphys, the helmsman, kept the ship as close as possible to the Thracian shore of the peninsula called the Chersonese, because Laomedon, the King of Troy on the easterly side, was hostile to all Hellenic ships. In the darkness the Argonauts rowed through unobserved and came safely into the sea of Marmora, or as it was called then the Propontis. With a fair wind they reached the peninsula of the Dolimonians, whose King Kyzikos was celebrating his wedding to Kleite. Kyzikos invited the Argonauts to join in the festivities and while these were in progress the guards left on board the *Argo* were attacked with rocks and clubs by six-headed giants known as the Earthborn, who came from the interior. Herakles had stayed behind with the guards and with his arrows he slew them one by one.

After the wedding festivities the Argonauts sailed away for the Bosphorus, but a fierce north-east gale swept down and they were making so little progress that Tiphys the helmsman thought it prudent to turn the ship about and make for the lee of the peninsula they had left. In the confusion of the storm Tiphys lost his bearings and the *Argo* was beached. It was a pitch-dark night and suddenly the Argonauts were attacked by armed warriors. A sharp battle ensued; it was only after some of the enemy had been killed and the rest driven off that the Argonauts discovered they had been fighting with their kindly hosts who had mistaken the Argonauts for raiders. To their bitter sorrow the Argonauts found that the noble King Kyzikos had himself been killed. His funeral rites, in which the Argonauts took part, lasted for three days, but when at the end of them the Argonauts sought to leave this tragic spot they were weather-bound for another twelve days. On the twelfth night, while they were all asleep except for two sentries, a kingfisher hovered over Jason's head, twittering. Mopsos, one of the sentries, who understood the language of birds, knew it was announcing that the wind had dropped.

On the way to the mouth of the Bosphorus Herakles challenged the Argonauts to a contest of strength, the victor to be the one who could row the longest. At the end of several hours the only ones still able to handle an oar were Jason, Kastor and Polydeukes (Castor and Pollux), the heavenly twins, and Herakles himself. Then Kastor's strength began to fail and Polydeukes, afraid that his brother might over-do it, shipped his own oar and gave up. Jason and Herakles were now the only two of the Argonauts pulling away at their oars. Then just as they reached the mouth of a river on the Asiatic shore Jason fainted, and a second or two later Herakles's oar broke, and half of it was carried away by the sea. Herakles fell backwards off his bench and was so much annoyed that it looked for a moment as if he were going to lay the other half of his oar about the shoulders of his companions, who hurriedly put their own oars through the holes and managed to

44

beach the *Argo* beside the bank of a river.

The people of Mysia in whose country they had landed received the Argonauts warmly and provided them with the food they badly needed. Herakles, still angry at the way his oar had broken, did not eat anything but went off into the woods to find a tree from which he could cut himself a new oar. He uprooted a great pine and dragged it back to the camp fire in order to fashion his oar. When he called for his young squire Hylas to come and help him, Hylas did not answer. Herakles was told that an hour ago the youth had gone to fetch water from a spring not far away. When he did not come back Polyphemos had started off to look for him.

Herakles, shouting for Hylas, hastened in the direction of the spring and met Polyphemos brandishing his sword.

"My friend, I have bad news for you," Polyphemos said. "Hylas went to the spring of Pegae and has not returned. Either he has been attacked by robbers or by wild beasts, for I heard him cry."

Polyphemos led Herakles to the spring, and there beside it was the bronze ewer which Hylas had meant to fill with water. Herakles was in despair, for he was devoted to Hylas. He and Polyphemos went shouting everywhere for the boy and if they met any of the country folk they made them join in the search. It was useless. Hylas was nowhere to be found. And he never would be found. The water-nymphs of Pegae had been so much charmed by the beauty of Hylas that they had pulled him down through their water to a grotto beneath, where they kept him to be their playmate.

When dawn came, a favouring breeze had sprung up and Tiphys called on the Argonauts to get aboard quickly and make the most of it.

"But where are Herakles and Polyphemos?" they cried.

"We cannot wait for them," Jason said.

At this Telamon, the father of the mighty Ajax, accused Jason of trying to get his own back on Herakles because he had been defeated by him in the rowing contest. The argument grew fiercer and it looked as if the question whether to take advantage of the wind and leave Herakles and Polyphemos would never be settled when from the depths of the sea Glaukos, the wise interpreter of the sea-god Nereus, rose and seized the *Argo*'s keel.

"Herakles has still to complete the Labours he must perform for Eurystheus before he is taken to dwell with the Immortals. Let there be no vain regret for him. Polyphemos is destined to found a city here in Mysia. Those two are wandering in search of Hylas, but a divine nymph will make Hylas her husband and he will be happy."

With these words Glaukos plunged down again into the sea and the Argonauts ceased to quarrel with one another.

And here we have to leave the Argonauts and follow Herakles back to Mycenae to be told by Eurystheus what was to be his next task.

The Stables of Augeias

PROBABLY Eurystheus thought he would pay Herakles out for going off with the Argonauts. At any rate when Herakles arrived in Mycenae to hear what his fifth task was to be, he was told that it was to clean the stables of Augeias in one day.

This king of Elis had more cattle than anybody in Hellas because they were immune from every malady that affects cattle. It was believed that this privilege had been granted to him by his father Poseidon. Augeias had three hundred black bulls with white legs, two hundred red bulls, and innumerable cows. He also had twelve white bulls with extra long horns which protected the herds by driving off any wild beasts that attacked them. For some reason or other, which history does not relate, the stables and cattle yards had not been emptied of dung for many years. This did not affect the health of the cattle but it did cause what was probably an outbreak of typhoid all over the Peloponnese. Moreover, some of the valley pastures were so deep in dung that they could not be ploughed.

Eurystheus chuckled to himself at the notion of Herakles carrying dung away on his shoulders in basket after basket and at the end of the day finding he had hardly made any impression on the great heaps of dung.

47

Herakles arrived in Elis with his nephew Iolaos, who was acting again as his squire since the loss of Hylas.

"If I clear up the mess your cattle have made before night will you make a tenth of your cattle over to me ?"

Augeias roared with laughter.

"I don't think you'll be able to do that, but I don't object to your trying. However, if you're going to claim any of my cattle as a reward you must swear an oath by the head of Zeus, the father of gods and men, that you will have all the dung cleared by nightfall."

Herakles did something he had never done before and never did again. He swore an oath by Zeus, the father of gods and men, after King Augeias had sent for his eldest son Phyleus to witness the oath. Then Augeias in his turn swore an oath to give Herakles a tenth of his cattle if he was successful in doing what he had sworn to do. A minute or two after Augeias had sworn his oath one of the twelve white guardian bulls mistook Herakles for a real lion and lowering its head charged at him. Iolaos shouted a warning but he need not have been alarmed; Herakles caught hold of the bull's left horn and twisted its neck until it collapsed on the ground. The bravest Spanish matador could not perform a feat of strength like that to-day.

With the help of Iolaos Herakles then diverted the course of the river Alpheios so that it ran through the stables and the yard and on down into the valley pastures and by nightfall there was no dung left.

The Stables of Augeias

Eurystheus had sent Kopreus, his herald, to Elis for the pleasure of hearing from him what a mess Herakles had made of himself trying to empty the stables of dung. Kopreus told Augeias that Herakles had been set to cleanse the stables as one of the Labours he was bound to perform. So, when instead of claiming a tenth of the cattle Herakles claimed the twelve white guardian bulls, Augeias refused to hand them over and what is more had the audacity to deny that he and Herakles had ever made a bargain.

Herakles had set his heart on having those twelve white bulls, and demanded that the argument between him and Augeias should be decided by judges duly appointed. Herakles called on the son of Augeias to testify, and Phyleus testified that his father had indeed sworn an oath to let Herakles have a tenth of his cattle if he succeeded in cleaning the stables in a single day. In a rage Augeias banished both Herakles and his own son from Elis. It was true, he admitted, that he had made a bargain with Herakles, but it was not he who had cleansed the stables. It was the river-god Alpheios.

So Herakles had to go back to Mycenae without the cattle he had fairly won, and to complete his chagrin Eurystheus refused to count this as one of the ten Labours because he argued that Herakles had made a business deal with Augeias. You will remember that Eurystheus had refused to accept the destruction of the Lernaean hydra because Herakles had been helped by Iolaos. So this would mean seven more Labours for Herakles to accomplish before he would be free of taking orders from Eurystheus.

"You will now rid the Stymphalian marsh of the birds that are terrorizing the country round it," the herald ordered.

Herakles had no alternative but to obey.

The Stymphalian Birds

THE Stymphalian birds were a kind of crane or ibis or spoon-bill, with beaks and claws of brass and brazen-tipped feathers. Some said that they were man-eaters but this seems improbable. What they did when they rose in a great flock from the marsh where they had been wading was to drop a shower of their feathers, the brazen tips of which often killed the people they struck.

When Herakles reached the marsh, which was surrounded by a dense forest, he wondered how he was going to deal with the birds. He could not walk over the morass nor could he cross it in a boat because there was not enough water. In any case he did not have enough arrows to kill such a multitude.

While Herakles was sitting by the edge of the marsh, trying to think of a way to perform his task of driving these horrible birds far away from Arcadia, the goddess Athene suddenly appeared. He bowed his head before those lustrous grey eyes and bent his knees in worship.

"I knew that you would be puzzled how to accomplish the task you have been set, and so I begged father Zeus to let me ask Hephaistos to make a brass rattle. Here it is."

Herakles took the rattle Athene offered him.

"This rattle makes such a noise that when you sound it these noxious birds will be terrified and will fly away to escape from the noise," he was assured.

When Herakles spoke his gratitude Athene had vanished but the brass rattle was still in his hand.

Herakles climbed up the lower slopes of Mount Kyllene, which overlooked the marsh, and began to shake his rattle. Even he was startled at first by the terrific noise it made. Earth and sky seemed to shake at the sound. If people had rattles like this at football matches to-day both teams would rush off the field in terror.

The Stymphalian birds rose in one flock and flew away as fast as they could to escape from the noise of that rattle.

"Well, well," Herakles chuckled to himself. "That is the lightest Labour I have accomplished yet."

The Stymphalian birds were said to be under the protection of Ares, the god of war, and perhaps that is why they flew as far as the island of Ares off the south coast of the Black Sea.

Some time after they arrived there the *Argo*, which had had a tough time getting through the Bosphorus, was sailing toward the island of Ares before a light breeze when at dusk the breeze left them, and they had to row past the island to find a place to anchor for the night. Suddenly one of those Stymphalian birds hovered over the *Argo* and let fly one of its feathers. The brazen tip struck the shoulder of one of the Argonauts called Oileus, and the unexpected blow made him drop his oar. His companion on the bench drew out the feather and bound up the wound. When a

second bird came swooping on the ship, another of the Argonauts managed to shoot it down into the sea.

Apparently the tale of how Herakles had driven the birds away from Arcadia had reached the Argonauts. One of them, called Amphidamas, suggested that they should try to scare the birds away by noise.

"Put on your helmets," he advised. "Then half of you row by turns and half fence the ship round with spears and shields. Then all together shout as loudly as you can to scare the birds. When we reach the island we'll make still more noise by clashing our shields together."

This they did when they landed. The noise frightened the birds, which flew around at first in alarm. Then the Argonauts made a roof of shields above their heads so that the brass-tipped feathers fell harmlessly, and in the end, unable to stand the noise the Argonauts were making, the birds flew away southward to the mountains of the Caucasus.

The Cretan Bull

AFTER Herakles came back from what seemed such an easy success with the Stymphalian birds, Eurystheus was determined to make the Labours he still had to undergo more difficult. So far Herakles had been set tasks on the Peloponnese, not so far away. For the Seventh Labour Eurystheus commanded him to bring the Cretan bull to Mycenae.

The bull Herakles was sent to capture was a ferocious beast with flames coming out of its nostrils. It was doing a great deal of damage in the island of Crete by knocking down the walls of orchards and uprooting the fruit-trees.

When Herakles arrived in Crete, King Minos offered to help him in every way; but Herakles knew that if he accepted such help Eurystheus would claim that the Seventh Labour had not been fulfilled any more strictly than the Second and the Fifth. Herakles decided to tackle the bull himself. It gave him as tough a tussle as he had ever had, but in the end he managed to overcome it and bring it back with him to the mainland of Hellas in a ship. When the bull was shown to Eurystheus it seemed so mild that Eurystheus dedicated it to Queen Hera and set it free.

Hera was furious at having the fruit of one of Herakles's Labours dedicated to her, and she promptly drove the bull mad.

It rushed about in the neighbourhood of Sparta, doing a lot of damage. Then Hera sent it to Arcadia where it did more damage. Finally she sent it across the Isthmus of Corinth to Marathon in Attica. She probably wanted to annoy Athene. If so she failed, because Theseus dragged it to Athens and sacrificed it to Athene.

The next Labour that Eurystheus set Herakles was a formidable one indeed. It was to harness to a chariot and drive back from Thrace to Mycenae the four man-eating mares of King Diomedes. Some say that Herakles performed this task alone but others more probably say that he called for volunteers to help him. What is certain is that he started off alone for Thrace, because on his way we know that he stayed with his friend Admetos of Pherae.

When I was in my early 'teens I read Euripides' play *Alkestis* and before we hear how Herakles tackled those man-eating mares I must tell her story.

Alkestis

APOLLO had a son called Asklepios (the Romans called him Aesculapius) who was sent as a boy to the wise centaur Cheiron to learn the art of medicine and when he grew up he became so skilful a physician that he was able to restore the dead to life. Pluto complained to his brother Zeus that some of his subjects in the Underworld were being stolen from him, and that Asklepios had been paid for doing this. Zeus in a fit of rage struck Asklepios with a thunderbolt. Later he restored Asklepios to life and granted him divine immortality, when he was worshipped by the ancient Greeks as the father of medicine.

When Zeus struck Asklepios with that thunderbolt Apollo was furious, but he did not dare quarrel directly with Zeus. However, he killed the Cyclops who had forged the thunderbolt. Zeus punished him for this by banishing him for a year from Olympus to serve a mortal, but the sentence was lightened as much as possible by choosing for Apollo's master the kindhearted Admetos, King of Pherae.

Admetos treated Apollo with reverence and was grateful for the way Apollo made his cattle flourish. Apollo on his side was grateful to Admetos for the way he had made his year of servitude as agreeable as possible. Anxious to reward him he enquired of

E

the Fates about his future. He was distressed to hear from them that Admetos had only a short time to live. The Fates were three sisters who spun the life of an individual. Clotho held the distaff; Lachesis spun the thread; Atropos cut it short.

Apollo plied the Fates with wine under the influence of which they consented to let Admetos remain alive longer if he could persuade somebody from his family to die in his stead. Apollo told Admetos what the Fates had decided, and the latter said he was sure that his father would be willing to die for him. He had often heard him complain about the burden of old age. However, when Admetos begged his father to die for him, the old gentleman declared that, although he had sometimes grumbled about the aches and pains and discomfort of old age, he had no desire to die. Nor was the mother of Admetos more willing to leave this world.

It was then that Alkestis, the beautiful wife of Admetos, volunteered to die for him. I remember when we read Euripides' play at school that I was rather shocked by the apparent readiness with which Admetos accepted his wife's offer. She, by the way, was a daughter of King Pelias of Iolkos, and so a first-cousin of Jason the Argonaut.

The lovely and devoted Alkestis took poison so that her husband might live.

The mourning for his dead wife had just begun when Herakles arrived in Pherae on his way to Thrace. Admetos did not want his old friend to feel an intruder at such a moment. He did not tell him that somebody as near and dear to him as Alkestis had died.

He pretended that it was a guest who had come for a brief visit. So Herakles was welcomed with all the hospitality for which Admetos was famous.

Herakles soon found out that the mourning was not for any stray guest but for Alkestis. He was deeply touched by the way Admetos had tried to spare his embarrassment over arriving at such a sad time, by pretending that it was only some stray guest who had died. He made up his mind to wrestle with Thanatos when he came to take Alkestis away to Hades. It was believed that Thanatos, which in Greek means Death, was a tangible figure that literally carried away the dead. So Herakles watched by the tomb of Alkestis for Thanatos to come for her and carry her down to Hades, and when the dread figure came Herakles wrestled with him and compelled him to release Alkestis. So Alkestis was brought back to life and Herakles could feel that he had repaid the hospitality of a bereaved host, who had not allowed his own sorrow to interfere with that hospitality.

When Herakles quitted that house of rejoicing which he had entered as a house of mourning, he must have felt the part he had played in making that change was a good omen for the successful performance of his Eighth Labour.

The Mares of Diomedes

D IOMEDES was a son of Ares and king of the fierce Bistonians in Thrace. His city was Tirida, of which no trace has been found to-day.

We do not know how Diomedes obtained these savage mares. They were kept tethered with iron chains to bronze mangers, and fed with unfortunate visitors.

When Herakles reached Tirida he went at once to the stables. He used his club to knock out all the grooms except a youth called Abderos. With the help of Abderos he drove the mares down to the sea; there he left them among the sand-dunes.

By this time Diomedes had mustered some of his warriors to go in pursuit of his mares. Herakles, remembering what he had done with the river Alpheios, cut a way through the sand-dunes for the sea to flow in over the low-lying land beyond. The Bistonian warriors turned to avoid the water. Herakles pursued them and stunned Diomedes with his club. Then he dragged his senseless body round what had become a lake until he came to the dunes where he had left the mares. The mares, supposing it was their regular meal, gobbled up their owner. Herakles looked round for young Abderos, only to find that the mares had already eaten him up too.

The mares were so full of food by now that they became quite docile, and Herakles led them back into Tirida. Although they had never been harnessed before he decided to harness them to the chariot of their late master. This he succeeded in doing. The fierce Bistonians were so much impressed by the hero's feat of arms and display of skill that they loaded the chariot with provisions when he announced his intention of driving it over hill and dale to Mycenae.

And drive the chariot to Mycenae he did, through the wilds of Thrace, down into Thessaly past Mount Olympus, past Mount Ossa, past Mount Pelion, on through Boeotia to Thebes, from Thebes down to Attica over the Isthmus of Corinth and on until he drove into the market-place of Mycenae.

Eurystheus was so frightened when he saw the man-eating mares that he could hardly bring himself to raise the lid of the pot in which he used to hide himself, in order to say,

"The mares must be set free on Mount Olympus and offered to Queen Hera."

Nobody in Mycenae seemed anxious to drive the mares to Mount Olympus, and at last Herakles himself had to take them there. This led to a report generally believed that Herakles himself had offered them to Hera. This used to annoy him because he did not feel in the least anxious to propitiate Hera.

The Girdle of Hippolyte

EURYSTHEUS must have been wondering and talking over what was to be the next Labour for Herakles when his daughter Admete suggested, perhaps only half in earnest, that Herakles should be told to bring back for her the golden girdle which Ares had given to Hippolyte, one of the Queens of the Amazons.

Herakles called for volunteers and among others who sailed with him were Peleus, the father of Achilles, and Telamon, the father of Ajax, those two great heroes of the Trojan war. Both Peleus and Telamon had been Argonauts and no doubt Herakles was glad to have them with him for a similar voyage.

The country of the Amazons stretched back from the southern shores of the Black Sea into what is now Armenia. At one time these female warriors had been much more numerous and their territory much more widely spread, but now they dwelt in their cities round the mouth of the river Thermodon, the queens of which were Hippolyte, Antiope and Melanippe.

The ship that Herakles took through the Hellespont and the Bosphorus had a much easier voyage than the *Argo*, as far as the weather went. The mouth of the river Thermodon was safely reached and the anchor was dropped in the port of Themiskyra,

the city ruled by Queen Hippolyte, who herself offered a warm welcome to Herakles. Indeed the Amazon was so strongly attracted to the hero that she was making up her mind to offer him the golden girdle of Ares as a sign of her affection.

Hera was angry when she thought that Herakles was going to find his Ninth Labour so easy. Moreover, when Herakles had brought the mares of Diomedes to Olympus and made it clear to the goddess that it was Eurystheus not himself who was offering the mares to her, her anger against him had been rekindled. So now Hera disguised herself in the dress of an Amazon made from the skins of wild beasts, and carried the brass bow and the shield shaped like a half moon. Then she went about spreading a rumour that Herakles and his companions were planning to carry off Hippolyte to Hellas and demand a heavy ransom for her. The Amazons in a rage mounted their horses and charged down upon the ship, shooting their arrows as they charged. Herakles supposed that Hippolyte had come aboard the ship in order to betray him. He seized her axe and killed her with it, and one after another he and his companions killed the Amazons who were trying to board the ship.

It was long afterwards before Herakles found out the trick that Hera had played. At the time he was sure that Hippolyte had meant to kill him and you must remember that the Amazons were as formidable fighters as any men.

On his way back to Mycenae, as the ship was passing through the Hellespont, Herakles saw by the Trojan shore what at first he

thought was a marble statue. He gave orders to pull in closer and then he saw that the statue was in fact a young woman chained to a rock with nothing to cover her except a necklace of jewels. Herakles swam ashore and set her free. She told him that she was Hesione, a daughter of Laomedon the King of Troy, and that an oracle had told her father to leave her thus to appease Poseidon, who had sent a sea-monster to devour the people dwelling on the plain beside the sea, and to spurt sea-water over their fields and spoil the crops. Poseidon had done this because her father had failed to sacrifice the cattle he had promised in gratitude for the help Poseidon had given him in building the walls of Troy.

So Herakles went up to the city and volunteered to destroy the monster if Laomedon would give him the two white horses which Zeus had given to Laomedon to make up for his carrying away the beautiful Trojan youth called Ganymede. Zeus had descended in the shape of an eagle and had flown off with Ganymede to Olympus, where he made him the cup-bearer of the gods in place of his own daughter Hebe.

The reason why Herakles wanted those two white horses was that they were immortal and could gallop over water and over corn as if they were as light as wind. They were in fact the first example of the hovercraft of to-day.

Laomedon agreed to the reward Herakles asked and the goddess Athene, who suspected that Queen Hera was seeking to involve Herakles in a disaster, advised him to have a high wall built on the plain. On this Herakles waited. When the monster came out of the sea to go spurting salt water over the fields, it saw Herakles and came towards the wall, its huge jaws wide open. Herakles at once jumped down its throat, and for three days in the monster's belly he hacked away with his sword until at last he managed to slay it. Jonah had a more peaceful time when he was swallowed by a whale.

Laomedon thanked Herakles for his feat in destroying the monster and presented him with what Herakles supposed were the two immortal white horses.

When Herakles arrived back in Mycenae he handed the golden girdle of Hippolyte to Eurystheus's daughter, Admete, who was naturally very proud of it. Eurystheus, too, was pleased because he thought the golden girdle would be a valuable addition to her dowry and win her a good marriage. He also coveted some rich robes Herakles had taken from the Amazons.

"No, no," Herakles told him. "I am going to present them to the Temple of Apollo at Delphi."

Eurystheus was inclined to send Herakles away at once on his Tenth Labour but he was afraid of offending Apollo and grudgingly agreed to let Herakles go to Delphi before he returned to hear what his Tenth Labour was to be.

Besides taking the robes to the Temple at Delphi Herakles intended to take the two immortal white horses to Olympus so that they could mate with the mares of Diomedes. You can imagine his rage when he found that Laomedon had cheated him and that the two white horses he had brought from Troy were not the immortal pair. He made up his mind that when he had finished his Twelve Labours he would lead an expedition to Troy and punish King Laomedon for cheating him. However, he left the two mortal horses to mate with the mares of Diomedes and there were still wild horses on Mount Olympus until the time of Alexander the Great, hundreds of years later.

The Red Cattle of Geryon

WHEN Herakles returned from Olympus to hear from Eurystheus what his next Labour was to be he was told that he must find and bring back with him the red cattle of Geryon.

"The red cattle of Geryon?" Herakles repeated. "What in the name of Zeus will you be asking me to do next?"

"Commanding not asking," Eurystheus corrected with a malicious smile.

Herakles said no more and set out upon his Tenth Labour.

Geryon was more of a monster than a man. He had three bodies with six arms and three heads, but only one pair of legs. He lived far away somewhere at the western end of the world on an island that was the colour of the sunset, called Erytheia. Here, Geryon kept his herd of cattle, which were guarded by Eurytion, his herdsman, and Orthros, a savage two-headed dog, a brother of three-headed Cerberus, the watch dog of Hades, the Hellhound, of whom we shall hear more later.

The oldest legend says that Herakles sailed to Erytheia across the stream of Okeanos in a golden goblet lent to him by Helios, the god of the Sun. When he landed on the island he was immediately attacked by Orthros. Herakles banged him on each head with his club and that was the end of the watch dog. Then he banged Eurytion the herdsman on the head, and finished him off.

Geryon now appeared on the scene and Herakles shot him through all three bodies with one of his poisoned arrows. It was believed that the arbutus sprang from the drops of his blood. This seems improbable because, although the strawberry-shaped fruit of the arbutus may have an insipid taste, it is not at all poisonous.

Herakles now embarked with Geryon's cattle in the golden goblet and, using his lion's skin as a sail, he reached south-west Spain. That was the oldest story, but the later story was that Erytheia was the site of the city of Gades, the Cadiz of to-day. Here the pasture on which those red cattle fed was so rich that their milk produced only curds without any whey. I feel sure that the later story was the true one.

There has been a lot of argument about whether the Pillars of Hercules, as we call the Straits of Gibraltar to-day, were two mountains on either side of the Straits or actually two brass columns said to have been erected by Herakles himself at Gades, at which sailors safely home from a voyage were accustomed to offer sacrifices to Herakles himself after he became immortal.

We do not know who accompanied Herakles when he started to drive Geryon's red cattle from Gades to Mycenae, but we do know that the effort occupied him for months and months. When he left Gades he went up through Spain and crossed the Pyrenees into Gaul. When he reached the territory of the Ligurians, which is what to-day we call the Riviera, and the country inland, two

Ligurians who were reputed to be sons of Poseidon tried to steal the cattle and Herakles killed both of them. Ligys, their elder brother, then attacked Herakles and his small band of followers with a strong Ligurian force. The battle was fierce, and Herakles used up all the arrows in his two quivers. To make matters worse, the ground was rich and soft and there was not a stone to be found for the slingers.

Herakles was in despair. Utterly exhausted and wounded he fell on his knees and with tears in his eyes besought his father Zeus to help him. Zeus heard his prayer and cast a heavy cloud over the battle-field, from which poured a hail of stones which put the Ligurians to flight. If you ever find yourself between Marseilles and the mouth of the great river Rhône you can see a plain about fifteen miles inland which is still strewn with stones of the right size for slings; they are said to be the remains of the shower of stones that saved the day for Herakles.

Herakles crossed the Alps with Geryon's cattle, meaning to reach what we now call the Tyrol and go on south along the eastern side of the green Adriatic to reach Hellas. But he took the wrong road and came south into Italy. He reached the river Tiber and was welcomed by Evander, an exile from Arcadia, who was living in the Aventine forest. The Aventine would one day be one of the famous seven hills of Rome, but Rome was still very many years from being founded.

The menace of the Aventine forest was a monster called Cacus. He had three heads and could blow fire from his three mouths.

The Red Cattle of Geryon

He lived in a deep cave outside which the skulls of the people he had killed were nailed up over the entrance and inside the floor was strewn with human bones. One evening Herakles had driven his cattle across the Tiber and, tired out, lay down to sleep on the grassy bank. During the night Cacus stole two of the bulls and four of the heifers from the herd and dragged them backwards by their tails into his cave.

Herakles woke up at break of day and looked everywhere for the missing cattle, but he could not find them and at last decided to give them up for lost and drive the rest of the herd onward south. Then suddenly he heard the faint lowing of one of the stolen heifers, and following the direction of the sound he found the cave. The entrance was barred by a large rock which a dozen ordinary men would have found too heavy to move at all; Herakles pushed it aside with one hand, rushed into the cave, seized Cacus and battered his three heads to pieces.

Herakles then built an altar to Zeus, at which he sacrificed one of the bulls stolen by Cacus. Then he freed Evander from the annual tribute he had been forced to pay the Etruscans, and at last was able to drive Geryon's cattle further on south, still under the impression that he was driving them along the right road for Hellas.

The Romans used to claim that Hercules, as they called him, founded the cities of Pompeii and Herculaneum on his way southward, but we can hardly believe that he bothered to found cities when he was so much preoccupied with getting those red cattle

73

safely to Mycenae.

He kept on driving them further south until he reached Rhegium, the Reggio of to-day, in the toe of Italy. One night he found that the ratcheting of the cicadas in the trees was so loud that he could not get to sleep. He begged the gods to silence them and they did. Hera may have been annoyed by the way the other Olympians bothered to pay attention to Herakles's disturbed night. Anyway she was responsible for making one of his bulls leave the herd and go plunging into the sea to swim across the narrow strait to Sicily.

Herakles swam after it and found it where it was hiding itself among the herds of Eryx, the king of the mountain of that name. Eryx was a son of Aphrodite and believed himself to be immortal. He was a great boxer and wrestler and challenged Herakles to a contest. Herakles said he would accept the challenge if Eryx would stake his kingdom against the runaway bull. Herakles won all the bouts of boxing and when the wrestling match started Herakles lifted Eryx up over his head and dashing him to the ground killed him. He did not intend to kill him; indeed, he had supposed that Eryx as the son of a goddess really was immortal. As a result of this contest Herakles won the kingdom of Eryx, but his immediate task was to get Geryon's cattle to Mycenae and he made the kingdom over to its inhabitants until one day a son of his own should come from Hellas to claim it. Years later that is what happened when a descendant of Herakles founded a Greek colony there.

The Red Cattle of Geryon

Herakles drove the cattle on through Sicily, but when he reached Syracuse he found he could not get a ship to take him and the cattle to Hellas; so he drove them back across the strait and then took them northward along the east coast of Italy. His object was to do what he had intended to do first. That was to drive the herd down the other side of the Adriatic and on down through the Epirus to the south side of the Corinthian gulf, and finally by way of the Isthmus to reach Mycenae with them.

Unfortunately when Herakles got his cattle to the Adriatic Gulf and was preparing to turn south Hera had one more of her fits of malice against him and sent a gadfly to stampede the cattle into rushing east across Thrace. Finally Herakles managed to dam the River Strymon and get the cattle across it.

So at last Herakles reached Mycenae and was able to hand over to Eurystheus that herd of Geryon's red cattle which he had been successful in driving right across Europe.

"Well," he said to Eurystheus, "I have finished my Ten Labours and I must say this Tenth Labour was the toughest of the lot. They have taken me eight years and one month. I think I am entitled to a rest."

"Oh, but as I told you, I do not recognize your Second Labour, when you were helped by Iolaos nor your Fifth when you hired yourself out to Augeias. Moreover, you were bound over to serve me for twelve years, so I have a right to impose two more Labours upon you. And the first of these is to bring me some of the golden apples of the Hesperides. Your geography is not good or you would not have taken such a long time to find yourself back in Hellas from the western edge of the world. We do not know exactly where the garden of the Hesperides is, but we do know that it is somewhere beyond the sunset and you were able to find Geryon's cattle somewhere beyond the sunset.''

"But that apple-tree was a present to Queen Hera from Mother Earth when she was married to Father Zeus,'' Herakles protested. ''Is it likely that Hera will let me pluck her golden fruit ?''

"Your Eleventh Labour is to bring me some of that golden fruit,'' Eurystheus insisted.

"Some say that the garden of the Hesperides is in the far west. Others say that it is in the land of the Hyperboreans,'' Herakles grumbled.

"The problem is yours to solve,'' Eurystheus told him.

The Golden Apples of the Hesperides

H ERAKLES was not anxious to spend as much time finding his way to the garden of the Hesperides as he had spent finding his way back to Hellas with Geryon's cattle. So he decided to ask Nereus, the sea-god with oracular powers, how he should be able to find that faraway garden and how, when he found it, he should be able to bring back some of its fruit.

Herakles went up along the eastern shores of the Adriatic and followed it round until he reached the mouth of the river Po. There the river-nymphs, who were daughters of Zeus, showed him the old sea-god fast asleep. He looked like a heap of sea-weed lying there but when Herakles caught hold of him Nereus kept changing into different kinds of animals and even at one point into a tree. However, Herakles clung on to him until at last the father of the Nereids decided to give Herakles the advice he sought. He directed him to where in Mauretania, as Morocco used to be called, the great Titan Atlas held up the Sky. This had been the punishment inflicted on him by Zeus when the Titans rebelled against the gods of Olympus and were defeated. The garden was tended by his three nieces, the daughters of the Titan Hesperus, but the tree itself was guarded by the dragon Ladon, which coiled itself round the trunk of the tree and never slept.

The Golden Apples of the Hesperides

Nereus warned Herakles not to pluck the golden apples himself but to persuade Atlas to give them to him.

"How shall I be able to do that?" Herakles asked doubtfully.

"You must offer to hold up the globe of the Sky for him while he is getting the apples for you."

So Herakles set out for the garden, and when he offered to give the Titan a rest from holding up the globe of the Sky if he could obtain three apples, Atlas was so glad to be relieved of his burden for a while that he agreed.

"But I fear Ladon," he said.

"I'll deal with Ladon," Herakles assured him, and as he said this he shot a poisoned arrow at the dragon and killed it.

Herakles now knelt and took the weight of the celestial globe on his own shoulders while Atlas went off for the apples which he told his three nieces to pluck. The ancient Titan was so glad to be able to walk about again without that mighty burden on his shoulders that he suggested taking the apples himself to Eurystheus if Herakles would agree to holding up the celestial globe for a few months until he returned.

Now, Nereus had warned Herakles that Atlas would try to unload the globe of the Sky on his shoulders, and that he must be very careful if he did not want to find himself left holding something a great deal heavier than any baby.

"I'll do that for you," he told Atlas, pretending to agree. "But just hold up the Sky for a minute or two while I get a pad for my head."

Atlas thought Herakles meant what he said, so putting the golden apples down he took up his burden again, whereupon Herakles quickly picked up the apples and hurried away as fast as he could.

Herakles decided to go back to Hellas by a different way from the one he had taken with the cattle of Geryon. He decided to cross Libya, the king of which was Antaios, a son of Poseidon and Mother Earth. He made a habit of challenging strangers to wrestle with him and when they were completely exhausted he used to kill them. Antaios himself could never be exhausted because he only had to touch the earth with his body to be as strong as ever. He was building a temple to his father Poseidon and he was collecting the skulls of his victims to serve as tiles for the roof. Antaios lived in a cave at the foot of a high cliff and his main diet was lions' flesh. He always slept on the bare ground so that while he slept his body should acquire more and more strength.

Before the wrestling match Herakles and Antaios discarded the lion-skins they both wore and then massaged themselves thoroughly. Herakles rubbed himself with olive-oil but Antaios poured hot sand all over himself. Antaios, realising that Herakles would be the strongest wrestler he had yet met, was afraid that merely touching the earth with the soles of his feet might not renew his strength fast enough.

Herakles did not know that the strength of Antaios was revived by touching the earth; his plan for the contest was to nurse his own strength and try to exhaust Antaios. He was astonished to see that when he flung him full length on the ground he came up again with muscles bigger and harder than before. When they grappled one another again Antaios threw himself down to the earth of his own accord and came up again as fresh as paint. Herakles now realised that his adversary was being revived by contact with his earthly mother. He changed his tactics and instead of throwing Antaios on the ground he lifted him above his head, and cracking his ribs one by one held him up until he ceased to breathe.

Tradition said that the city of Tingis, which we call Tangier to-day, was founded by Antaios, and I have sometimes wondered whether the original golden apples of the Hesperides were tangerine oranges, and whether that garden was once carpeted by that exquisite blue iris we call Iris Tingitana.

Herakles now took advantage of being where he was to visit the famous oracle of Zeus at Ammon, in the hope of hearing good counsel from his father Zeus; but Zeus was silent. So without having been able to get any advice from his divine father Herakles went south and founded a city he called Thebes in honour of his own native city, and that Thebes is still there to-day. The King of Egypt at this time was Busiris, another son of Poseidon.

Egypt had suffered from drought and famine for several years, and Busiris had sent for Greek seers to advise him what to do about the droughts. They assured him that the droughts would cease if every year he sacrificed a stranger in honour of Zeus. When Herakles arrived he allowed himself to be bound and led to the altar, but when Busiris raised the sacrificial axe Herakles burst out of his bonds, snatched the axe out of the hands of Busiris and killed him. After this he killed all the priests who were attending the sacrifice.

Probably Herakles went to consult the Oracle of Zeus Ammon again, after killing Busiris and the priests, to ascertain if his divine father was angry with him. We may suppose that the Oracle commanded him to go to the Caucasus and release Prometheus from his suffering. At any rate, taking with him those three golden apples, that is where he went.

When Zeus had been angry with the way human beings were behaving, compared with the admirable way they had behaved under his father Kronos or Saturn in the Golden Age, he had deprived them of fire. The Titan Prometheus had stolen fire from the smithy of Hephaistos on Olympus and brought it away with him in a dry stalk of fennel, to give to humanity. Zeus was enraged and ordered Hephaistos to bind Prometheus to a mountain in the Caucasus where every day a huge eagle tore at his liver which grew again during the night. This agony had lasted for years and Prometheus begged in vain to have his immortality taken from him and to die.

By now Zeus had repented of the cruel punishment he had inflicted on Prometheus and he chose Herakles to bring peace to the unhappy Titan. The hero shot the eagle through the heart, and Prometheus was set free.

When Herakles returned to Mycenae he gave the three golden

apples to Eurystheus who gave them back to him. Herakles would have liked to give them back to Hera because the golden tree had been her wedding present from Mother Earth. However, he felt it was hopeless for him to win Hera's friendship and he gave them to Athene; she gave them back to the three nymphs in the Garden of the Hesperides.

The Chaining of Cerberus

THE Twelfth and last Labour of Herakles was by far the most formidable that he had been set. When Eurystheus ordered him to bring up from Tartarus the three-headed watchdog Cerberus, he probably hoped that Herakles would never come back from the Underworld. He might well fear that after those twelve years of servitude Herakles would be a dangerous enemy.

Fortunately for the hero, Zeus allowed Athene and Hermes to guide him on the way to the Underworld. If you look at the map of Greece you will see three peninsulas as the bottom of the Peloponnese. The middle one was called Tainaron and at the southerly end of it there was a cave which was one of the entrances to the Underworld. With Hermes beside him Herakles came to the banks of the Styx after a very dark descent. Over this river the souls of the dead had to pass, ferried across by the disagreeable old ferryman Charon. He charged an obol for doing this, which one can roughly call a farthing. The Hellenes used to put an obol in the mouths of the dead when they were buried because otherwise Charon would not ferry them across the Styx.

When Charon saw Herakles he refused at first to take him on board his boat, but he was so much frightened by the hero's threats of what he would do to him if he did not take him aboard that he turned out of the boat the souls waiting to be ferried across and rowed Herakles across. For doing this Pluto kept him in chains for a whole year.

At last the hero reached the gloomy portals of the House of Hades, outside which some of Pluto's black cattle were grazing. Herakles thought it would be a kindly act if he slaughtered one of the cattle and gave the ghosts a drink of warm blood to cheer them up. This naturally annoyed Menoites, Pluto's herdsman, and he challenged Herakles to wrestle with him. The hero seized him round the waist and was crushing his ribs one by one when Persephone came out of the House of Hades and after greeting Herakles affectionately begged him not to kill Menoites.

Persephone was the daughter of Demeter, the corn goddess, and when Pluto had wanted to marry her Demeter had refused. Then when Persephone was gathering flowers in a Sicilian field Pluto had caused a particularly large and lovely flower to grow. The Koré or Maid, as she was usually called, had picked this flower, whereupon the earth had opened and Pluto appeared with his chariot and carried her down to the Underworld. Demeter had been overcome by grief, and at last persuaded Zeus to bring Persephone back to the earth above. She would have been able to stay there but unfortunately, as she had eaten in the Underworld (although it was only a few pomegranate seeds), she had to spend half her life below.

No doubt for Persephone Herakles was a breath of the air above that she was always longing for, and that would account for the

affectionate way in which she received him.

When Pluto came out Herakles at once asked his leave to carry away Cerberus. Pluto considered this daring request for a moment or two. It may be that Zeus had confided in that grim brother of his how he was hoping to deify his son Herakles one day, if he showed himself worthy of worship by his heroic deeds. At any rate, Pluto told Herakles that he was welcome to carry off Cerberus provided he undertook to bring him back to Tartarus, and also, he added, if Herakles could get the better of the Hellhound without using either his arrows or his club.

When Herakles had tackled Geryon's two-headed dog, Orthros, who was a brother of Cerberus, he had used his club to batter in each head. Cerberus was a tougher opponent, with its three heads and barbed tail. When it saw Herakles the three heads began to bark at once, and in the words of the great poet Virgil all Tartarus resounded with the noise, but luckily for Herakles the heads had only one throat between them. He gripped this throat with both hands and squeezed so hard that Cerberus finally surrendered to escape being choked.

Herakles somehow dragged the monstrous dog out of the Underworld and when it saw light at the end of the dark tunnel it began to struggle against being dragged out into the sunshine. Herakles had to use all his strength to prevent it from turning back into the darkness. However, he was at last successful in hauling Cerberus out into the open air, where the Hellhound barked in rage at what seemed to him the repulsive aspect of the world above. The ancients believed that the spittle which dropped from those three mouths produced the plant aconite, which is a deadly poison.

We are not told what Eurystheus said when he saw Cerberus and we are not told anything about Herakles's return journey to the Underworld to take Cerberus back. We may presume that in its anxiety to get out of the disgusting sunlight the Hellhound was docile on the way back to its gloomy home.

Cerberus had one weakness; he enjoyed eating honey cake. Many years after this the Trojan Aeneas, guided by the aged Sibyl or seer of Cumae, descended Avernus, in southern Italy, which was another entrance to Tartarus. Of Aeneas's encounter with the Hellhound the great poet Virgil wrote:

"Huge Cerberus made the Underworld resound with his three-throated bark as he crouched in his cavernous kennel. The Sibyl, seeing the bristling on his necks, broke a honey cake made of drugged meal. He opened his three mouths greedily and swallowed the three pieces flung to him. Then his monstrous body sank down and he fell asleep."

That was what was called 'a sop to Cerberus'.

Aeneas was wise; he was not as strong as Herakles.

Omphale

AFTER he was quit of his servitude to Eurystheus Herakles decided he would like to be married again and sought the hand of Iole, the beautiful daughter of Eurytos, king of Oichalia in Euboea. Eurytos had been his tutor in archery, but knowing what Herakles had done to his first wife in that horrible fit of madness he refused to give his daughter to his former pupil. Iphitos, his eldest son, unlike his three brothers had pleaded for Herakles to be accepted as a suitor. Not long after this Iphitos came to Tiryns in search of some lost cattle which Eurytos believed had been stolen by Herakles. Herakles took the young man up to the top of a tower and asked him if he could see the cattle grazing anywhere. Then in a burst of mad rage which his enemy Hera had cast over him he threw poor Iphitos down from the tower to his death.

Immediately Herakles came to his senses and repented bitterly of what he had done. He went to Neleus, the King of Pylos to be purified, but Neleus refused. Then Herakles asked the Oracle of Delphi what he must do to be purified of this murder he so deeply regretted. The Oracle bade him undergo another year of servitude, and Hermes sold him to Omphale, the Queen of Lydia, in what we to-day call Asia Minor. The three silver talents which Omphale paid for her slave were offered to the children of

89

Iphitos, but their grandfather Eurytos refused to let them accept the compensation.

Herakles was a very useful slave to Omphale. He got rid of various bandits and other objectionable people.

And then in the same way as a ridiculous rumour goes round to-day and sometimes gets into the newspapers, a ridiculous rumour went round Hellas that Omphale had made Herakles give up wearing his lion-skin and dress himself up like a woman with jewellery and a purple shawl. He had to teaze wool and spin threads with her handmaids and if he made a clumsy mistake his mistress used to give him a clout with her golden slipper. So the story went, and of course as you have probably already found out, the more improbable a bit of gossip is the more anxious people are to believe and repeat it.

Here is the origin of that rumour. One day when Omphale, with Herakles in attendance holding a golden parasol over her head, went to visit some vineyards, Pan looking down from a hill saw Omphale and immediately fell in love with her. He told the Oreads in whose company he was that Omphale was the only woman he had ever loved, and the mountain nymphs had a good laugh among themselves.

Meanwhile, after they had inspected the vineyards, Omphale and Herakles retired to a cool grotto and to amuse themselves exchanged clothes. Herakles put on her purple gown, which was much too small for him, and in putting it on he split the sleeves. Then they decided to have a siesta and lying down on two couches fell fast asleep. Instead of waking up to take some refreshment before returning to the queen's palace, they slept on until it was dark.

Then Pan came creeping in to the grotto, but not on tiptoe because with his goat's hooves he did not have any toes. However, he stepped across the grotto as quietly as he could. His idea was to find out on which couch Omphale was asleep and then to waken her and tell her he had fallen madly in love with her. He felt round in the dark and feeling a silk dress he supposed that this was Omphale. He touched her cheek gently to waken her and was much disconcerted to find he was touching a beard. At that moment Herakles woke up and with a mighty kick sent Pan sprawling across the grotto. Omphale, hearing the noise, jumped up and called for lights. When they were brought she and Herakles laughed and laughed to see Pan squatting there and rubbing the bruise on his behind from the kick Herakles had given him.

The only way Pan could pay the hero out was by spreading a rumour all over Hellas that what had merely been a joke of the moment was the regular behaviour of Herakles.

The silly tale did not worry Herakles. He was soon to show them in Hellas that he was not wearing women's clothes. The end of his penitential servitude was due. Before he left Lydia he killed a large man-eating serpent and the grateful Queen Omphale sent him back to Tiryns loaded with rich presents.

The Battle of the Giants

THE year Herakles had spent with Omphale in Lydia brought back memories of the way King Laomedon of Troy had cheated him over the two immortal white horses. When he returned to Tiryns he fitted out an expedition to punish him. He was anxious that Telamon should be with him again, and went to Salamis to invite him to join the expedition. Telamon was glad to see Herakles and at a feast he was giving he handed the golden bowl of wine to his guest and asked him to pour the first libation to Zeus. Herakles knew that Telamon's wife was soon going to have a child. So Herakles prayed to his father Zeus that Telamon should have a son with a skin as hard to pierce as his own lion-skin.

Almost immediately after the feast came to an end Ajax was born. Herakles wrapped the baby in his lion-skin to make him invulnerable. Years later, Ajax would grow up to rival Achilles as a warrior in the Trojan War.

When the six ships reached the coast of Troy the Hellenes disembarked and Herakles led them to assault the city. Laomedon had had no warning of the attack and he was soon shot down by one of Herakles's deadly arrows. So were all his sons except one, whom Herakles spared because he had protested against the way his father had cheated Herakles over the immortal white horses. This was Priam, who now became King of Troy, and if ever you are lucky enough to read the Iliad of Homer you will hear a great deal about Priam during that Trojan war, which lasted ten years.

While the ships were sailing back to Hellas Hera persuaded Hypnos, the Spirit of Sleep, to hypnotize Zeus into unconsciousness and while he was asleep ordered Boreas, the North Wind, to blow with fury. Anybody who has sailed about the Aegean in summer knows how fierce those sudden northerly gales can be. The storm raised by Boreas in obedience to Hera drove Herakles's ship far off course to the south, as far as the island of Cos, where our lettuces originally came from.

When Zeus woke up he was very angry. He knew Olympian gods were to be attacked almost at once by the Giants, and he knew also that unless a mortal came to their aid the Giants might overcome them. So he sent Athene to bring Herakles back from Cos in time to take his part in driving the Giants back from Olympus. Herakles pursued them to the Phlegraean Fields near Vesuvius, in southern Italy, where there was a final terrific battle.

These monsters came up from the Earth, hurling huge rocks and burning trees at what they called the 'new' gods. In the end the Giants were vanquished and were buried under volcanoes, some of which like Etna and Vesuvius are still active. Herakles was responsible for despatching some of the most ferocious of the Giants. From one of them, called Porphyrion, he saved Hera. All the Olympian gods and goddesses took part in the battle except

Demeter, who wept throughout. She was probably frightened for what might happen to her beloved daughter Persephone in the Underworld.

After the battle with the Giants Herakles fought several wars in the Peloponnese, but wars can become as boring to read about as to fight in, and I shall not go into the details. One of the wars Herakles fought was against Augeias, the King of Elis. He had made up his mind to pay Augeias out for the way he had swindled him over the Fifth Labour. After Herakles had sacked Elis he used the spoils to found the Olympic Games, which were to be held every four years in honour of his father Zeus. It is rather a solemn thought that three thousand years later the Olympic Games should still be held every fours years, though of course there was a long gap of time before they were revived.

Eurystheus began to fancy, with all these wars in the Peloponnese, that Herakles was planning to make himself High King of Mycenae and rule all the Argives in Argolis. So he decided to banish Herakles from Tiryns.

Herakles was tempted for a while to make war on Eurystheus, but he was warned against this by Zeus. Moreover, since Hera had been leaving him alone after he came to her rescue in the battle with the Giants, he thought it would be better not to offend her by stirring up trouble in Argolis, of which country she was the revered protectress.

So with a following of Arcadians Herakles sailed across the gulf of Corinth to Calydon.

Deianeira

THAT terrible fit of madness during which Herakles had killed his wife and small sons had made him afraid to marry again. Now, after twelve years, he felt a longing to have children of his own and when he came to Calydon he fell in love with Deianeira, the lovely daughter of King Oineus. Apart from her beauty Herakles admired her skill as a charioteer and felt that she would always sympathize with his warlike exploits.

One of the many suitors for Deianeira's hand was the river-god Acheloos, and Oineus was tempted to give him his daughter; but Deianeira herself had no desire at all to wed Acheloos. She disliked extremely his great beard, from which a stream of water was always pouring, and when Herakles came to Calydon she begged her father to hear his suit. Oineus consented to hear what Herakles had to urge on his own behalf, but insisted that Acheloos should be present.

The immortal river-god was able to change into a bull or a spotted snake, but he appeared as himself in a green cloak to hear his rival pleading his suit. Herakles asked Oineus if he would not be proud to boast that Zeus was his father-in-law.

"And this you will be able to do if I marry your daughter."

"But I am the father of all Greek rivers and streams,"

Acheloos protested, "and the Oracle of Zeus at Dodona has recognized this and ordered all strangers who come to Calydon to offer sacrifices to me. I don't believe you *are* the son of Zeus," he added to Herakles.

This of course put Herakles into a violent rage and he challenged the river-god to mortal combat. Acheloos at once flung off his green cloak and the two rivals sprang at each other; after wrestling together Herakles threw Acheloos on his back. The river-god immediately changed himself into a spotted snake and tried to glide away. Herakles was too quick for him and gripped his rival by the throat. Somebody who had strangled two snakes when he was a baby was not at all afraid of this snake. Acheloos realised as much, and quickly changing himself into a bull he lowered his head and charged Herakles. The hero stepped aside and caught the bull by its horns. Then exerting all his great strength he flung the bull to the ground with such violence that its horns were forced into the soil. Herakles then broke off one of the horns and the river-god, confessing himself beaten, plunged into the water. Herakles flung the broken horn after him. The Naiads picked it up and filled it with fruit and flowers, and it became the cornucopia or horn of plenty. Acheloos admitted later that he had been worsted by a better man, but he was always a bit ashamed of the scar left on his forehead by the broken horn and used to hide it by twining reeds and boughs of willow round his head.

So Herakles and Deianeira were married and lived happily in

Calydon for three years. Then one day at a feast a young kinsman of King Oineus was told to pour water over Herakles's hands before the next course. The boy in his nervousness upset the bowl over the hero's legs. In a moment of irritation Herakles boxed the boy's ears. He had not the least intention of seriously hurting him, but he forgot how strong he was, and to his sorrow the boy was killed by what he meant as no more than a light blow.

Herakles was so much upset by this fatal accident that he felt he must go into exile to atone for what he had done. He decided to live in Trachis at the head of the Gulf of Euboea.

On the way to Trachis Herakles and Deianeira came to the banks of the river Euenos, which was swollen with winter rains, making the crossing of it impossible for Deianeira. While Herakles was wondering what to do the centaur Nessos trotted up and offered to carry Deianeira over on his back if Herakles could manage to swim across himself. The hero accepted this offer and lifted his wife on to the centaur's back. Then he tossed his club and his bow over to the opposite bank and with his lion-skin and arrows plunged in. After a hard battle with the torrent he managed to get safely across. He was bending down to pick up his bow when he heard a terrified scream from Deianeira, and there was Nessos galloping away with her.

Herakles snatched an arrow from his quiver and, although by now Nessos was at least a quarter of a mile away, that poisoned arrow from the hero's bow pierced him to the heart. As Nessos lay dying, after pulling out the arrow, he told Deianeira to take

some of the blood from his wound and keep it carefully because if ever in the future she should fancy she was losing the love of Herakles she could win it back by smearing some of the blood on any garment she gave him to wear.

Deianeira believed what Nessos told her and somehow managed to fill a phial with the centaur's blood without letting Herakles know what she had done.

Trachis

FOR a long time Herakles lived happily in Trachis with Deianeira, and she gave him four sons and a daughter. He with his
Arcadians had various wars on hand from time to time, but the
details are all much the same.

One incident, however, at this time is worth telling because it
shows Herakles fighting in a way that he never did in any of his
other exploits. The ruler of the city of Itonos was a son of Ares,
the god of war, whose name was Kyknos. His hobby was to
challenge guests for a big prize to fight a chariot duel with him.
He always won these duels and used to cut off the heads of the
losers and decorate the temple of his father Ares with their skulls.

Apollo was angry with Kyknos because he had taken to stealing
cattle that were being sent for sacrifice to Delphi. The god told
Herakles that it was his duty to fight one of these chariot duels
and if possible kill Kyknos. Herakles could never resist any opportunity to display his fighting skill and he accepted the challenge.
It was agreed that Herakles should be allowed to send for Iolaos,
who had been his charioteer in some of his adventures. Then Ares
announced that he should be his son's charioteer. This caused
something of a stir on Olympus, and Athene told Herakles he
would be wise to do without his lion-skin on this occasion and to

put on the golden breast plate she had given him. Zeus ordered Hephaistos to give Herakles a specially strong shield. At the same time Zeus bade Athene go down and warn Herakles that, although he might kill Kyknos, he must be content only to defend himself against Ares.

Athene thought it was unfair to Herakles to let a god attack him and not allow him to attack a god. So she mounted the chariot beside Herakles and Iolaos, determined to intervene if Ares started to attack Herakles.

The two chariots were driven at one another at full speed and the force with which the spears of the combatants struck their shields threw both Herakles and Kyknos out of their chariots on to the ground. They were both quickly up again on their feet and after fighting for a while, spear against spear, Herakles drove his spear into his adversary's neck, and Kyknos lay dead.

Ares, angered by the death of his son, rushed at Herakles sword in hand and was wounded by him in the thigh. As the god of war lay prone Herakles was on the verge of wounding him again when Zeus stopped the fight with a thunderbolt. Athene then took Ares back to Olympus, leaving Herakles and Iolaos to strip the arms from the dead body, which they left to be buried by others.

Back in Trachis Herakles and Deianeira lived on happily, and whenever he returned from his various expeditions he seemed as fond of her as when they were first married.

Then one day two doves from the Oracle of Zeus at Dodona told Herakles that at the end of fifteen months he would either die or pass the rest of his life in undisturbed serenity and happiness.

Herakles was setting out on an expedition with his Arcadian warriors to punish King Eurytos of Oichalia for wrongfully exacting tribute from the people of Euboea. At any rate, that is what he told his Arcadians, but Deianeira got it into her head that the real reason behind the expedition was to capture Iole, whose hand in marriage her father Eurytos had once refused to Herakles.

When, just before he set out against Oichalia, Herakles told Deianeira of the message brought him from Dodona by the two doves, she began to worry more than ever because she feared that Herakles was going to lose his life in this war against Eurytos. She told herself that if he were victorious and brought Iole back with him to Trachis there was little chance of his spending the rest of his life in perfect domestic peace.

The Divine Immortality of Herakles

ERAKLES succeeded in capturing Oichalia and killing Eurytos and his sons, and in making Iole his captive. It is said that when her family was killed Iole tried to kill herself by jumping from the city wall, but was unsuccessful because the wind turned her skirts into a parachute and she landed without a bone broken.

Herakles sent Iole, escorted by other Oichalian women, to Trachis and asked Deianeira to send him by Lichas the shirt and cloak he wore on ceremonial occasions. He had just consecrated an altar to Zeus and was proposing to offer a sacrifice of thanksgiving for the capture of Oichalia.

When Deianeira saw how beautiful Iole was she was more afraid than ever that she might lose the love of Herakles. Then she bethought herself of that phial she had filled with the blood of Nessos. That was a certain preservative of her husband's love, the centaur had promised her.

Deianeira had woven a specially fine shirt which she was keeping as a surprise for Herakles when he came back to Trachis and offered a great thanksgiving sacrifice for his safe return. She unsealed the phial and soaked a piece of wool in the centaur's blood, with which she rubbed the shirt. Then she packed the shirt and the cloak in a chest and told Lichas to keep the shirt locked up until Herakles was ready to put it on. Lichas promised he would do as Deianeira asked and drove away in his chariot with the chest. A few minutes after he had left Deianeira happened to look at the piece of wool with which she had rubbed the shirt. She had thrown it away in the courtyard and to her horror she saw it burning away in the sunlight and deep crimson foam bubbling from the paving stones.

The unhappy Deianeira realised at once that Nessos had planned to revenge himself on Herakles one day and that the love-charm was in fact a deadly poison. She sent a courier to ride as fast as he could after Lichas and tell him to return, but the courier failed to overtake the chariot. Deianeira was frantic with grief for what she had done and vowed that if Herakles died through her folly she would kill herself.

Across the gulf on the north-west of Euboea the headland of Kenaion rose above the narrow stretch of water that separated the island from the mainland. Here was the marble altar Herakles had erected to his father Zeus in gratitude. Here was a throng of spectators reverently attentive to the ritual. Here was Herakles wearing that shirt woven for him by his wife, and here was a herd of cattle.

Herakles had sacrificed twelve of the finest bulls from this herd. He was pouring wine from a bowl on the altar after scattering grains of incense on the sacrificial fire when suddenly he gave a loud yell. The onlookers thought for a moment that he had been bitten by a snake. So he had in a way. The poison of the Lernaean hydra on the arrow with which Herakles had shot Nessos had begun to melt in the blood with which Deianeira had rubbed the shirt and was now running like fire through the blood of Herakles and burning up his flesh. The pain was frightful. In his agony Herakles screamed and overturned the altar. Then he tried to pull off the shirt but as he pulled his flesh came away with it and laid bare his very bones. His blood was seething now like water when red hot metal is dipped in it, and when Herakles plunged into the sea the sea boiled round him. Yet he swam on. When he reached the mainland he plunged into a stream which began to boil and remained hot for ever afterwards. It was called Thermopylae, which means 'Hot Gates'—the ever to be remembered Thermopylae where Leonidas and his three hundred Spartans died in their attempt to stem the invasion of the Persian host. And the hot stream is still there.

When Herakles came out of the boiling water he ran hither and thither, trying to escape from his agony, and as he ran he kept pulling trees up by the root. Then suddenly he saw Lichas hiding behind a rock and in a fury accused Lichas of trying to kill him. It was useless for Lichas to disown all responsibility for the fatal shirt. Herakles, picking him up, swung him three times round his head and threw him into the Euboean sea, where he was turned into a rock rising just above the waves in human shape. This rock was known as Lichas for long afterwards, and sailors avoided scrambling on to it because they thought it was still alive. They said it moved like a human body.

After this, Herakles reached Trachis and was lying in agony while his army lamented him when Iolaos sent Herakles's eldest son Hyllos, a boy of sixteen, and bade him take his father to Mount Oeta. Iolaos had been told by the Oracle of Delphi that Mount Oeta was the destined place for the death of Herakles.

When Hyllos came to his father, Herakles had only one idea in his head and that was to punish Deianeira before he died. Then Hyllos told him why Deineira had put the blood of Nessos on the shirt and that she had been so distraught by what she had done that she had stabbed herself and was now dead. Herakles knew that Deianeira was innocent, for he remembered a prophecy made by Zeus. 'No man alive will ever kill Herakles: he will be killed by a dead enemy.'

Hyllos now asked his father to give his final orders.

"Swear by the head of almighty Zeus, my son, that you will have me carried to the summit of this mountain and there burn me upon a funeral pyre of oak and wild-olive. Swear also, my son, that as soon as you come of age you will marry Iole."

And Hyllos swore the oath his father demanded of him.

Then Hyllos with his cousin Iolaos and other chosen companions carried Herakles to the very summit of Mount Oeta, and when the pyre had been made of oak-boughs and wild-olive they spread upon the top of it that lion-skin of Herakles and set there his club for a pillow. This done, Herakles mounted the pyre and ordered them to set fire to it. In spite of his commands none of them could bring himself to set the first torch against the pyre. In vain did Herakles call upon them to obey his command. They all held back. Then a shepherd called Poias, who was passing by, bade his son Philoktetes kindle the pyre. In the words of the Roman poet Ovid:

"As the pyre began to burn with hungry flames he spread the skin of the Nemean lion and with his club for a pillow he lay down, as happy an expression on his face as if, crowned with garlands among cups of wine, he were reclining on his couch at a banquet."

Out of gratitude to Philoktetes Herakles bequeathed to him his bow, his quiver and his arrows. If ever you read the history of the Trojan War you will hear that with one of those arrows Philoktetes killed Paris, the son of Priam, who by carrying off Helen from Sparta started that war.

While the flames were consuming the mortal part of Herakles a thunderbolt fell and the pyre became a heap of ashes. A cloud hid the ashes. Peal after peal of thunder rolled across the sky. When the cloud lifted there was no sign of Herakles. His immortal part, looking as majestic as his divine father, had been taken up to heaven by Zeus himself in his chariot drawn by four horses.

Zeus had told the Olympians that he was intending to take his son up to heaven and make him a god. When he asked if any of them disapproved of his intention he looked hard at Hera. She decided to give up the enmity and volunteered to adopt Herakles as a son. Zeus was very pleased.

"Now he is Herakles indeed," he declared.

Zeus had been a little worried about his plan to make Herakles one of the Twelve Olympians. He did not like the idea of expelling one of the existing Twelve. When he had made his son Dionysos one of the Twelve Hestia, whom the Romans called Vesta, had withdrawn voluntarily. So he was delighted when Hera suggested adopting Herakles, and what is more gave him her lovely daughter Hebe for a bride.

Hebe had once been the cupbearer of the Olympians and when Zeus had given this job to Ganymede she had felt rather superfluous. But Hebe was also the goddess of youth, and when she was married to Herakles she was always pleased to restore the youth of his best friends. Iolaos surprised everybody by suddenly appearing at a feast with the appearance of a young man of twenty.

Zeus decided to make Herakles the porter of Olympus, so that none of the other Eleven could feel he was taking the place of any of them. Herakles enjoyed being the porter of Olympus. He used to stand by the gates at dusk waiting for Artemis to come back from her hunting. When he found her chariot full of goats and hares he used to ask why she wasted her time killing such harmless animals when there were wild boars, wolves and lions to destroy. However, although he used to tease Artemis about killing hares he always enjoyed tucking into them.

I should like to go on and tell you about the various adventures of the sons of Herakles, known as the Heraklids, but it is time to bring my story to an end by letting you known that the behaviour of Eurystheus towards Herakles was avenged by Hyllos, the hero-god's eldest son. Eurystheus led an army in the Peloponnese against Athens, but he was defeated and Alkmene, the mother of Herakles, who was now a very old woman, had the pleasure of seeing the dead body of Eurystheus slain by her grandson.

Epilogue

Y o u may have thought sometimes when you were reading the story of Herakles that his exploits were not unlike those of Samson, and I want you to realise that Herakles was as much a real human being once upon a time as Samson.

The stories that people tell about us three thousand years hence will seem just as improbable as some of the stories we are told about people three thousand years ago. They will find it hard to believe that once upon a time great nations were planning to obliterate each other with atom bombs.

When we read about dragons and flying horses and gigantic serpents we must remember that those memories were kept alive by tales handed down of prehistoric monsters when human beings really did have to preserve themselves from dinosaurs and pterodactyls. When we read about the Nemean lion we must remember that in the dim and distant past a sabre-toothed tiger might make the neighbourhood extremely dangerous for people armed only with stones.

When boys and girls three thousand years hence read about Hitler they will wonder if such an evil monster like that could ever have really existed. Yet we know that he *did* exist.

I first read about those heroes of ancient Greece nearly eighty years ago and I am as much enthralled by their adventures now as I was when I first read about them.

One last word. I have used almost always the Greek spelling for the names of people and places. However, when some names were so familiar in their Latin form I have kept the Latin spelling of Olympus, Cerberus and one or two others. I felt that Olumpos and Kerberos would look too strange on the printed page. Our letter 'c' does not exist in the Greek alphabet. There is only 'k' or kappa, as it is called. You will notice how often 'ph', 'ps' and 'th' appear in Greek names. These are all letters of the Greek alphabet. 'Phi', 'psi', and 'theta'. And what is 'alphabet'? The two first letters of the Greek alphabet, alpha and beta. Even if you do not learn Greek it is worth learning the Greek alphabet. You will find it a great help with your spelling of so many English words, and also a great help for spelling chemical words.